THE
PATRÓN
WAY

side Story of
the World's Most Successful Tequila

THE PATRÓN WAY

From Fantasy to Fortune—Lessons on Taking
Any Business from Idea to Iconic Brand

ILANA EDELSTEIN

WITH

SAMANTHA MARSHALL

NEW YORK   CHICAGO   SAN FRANCISCO

LISBON   LONDON   MADRID   MEXICO CITY   MILAN

NEW DELHI   SAN JUAN   SEOUL   SINGAPORE

SYDNEY   TORONTO

1 2 3 4 5 6 7 8 9 0   DOC/DOC   1 9 8 7 6 5 4 3

ISBN   978-0-07-181764-6
MHID   0-07-181764-6

e-ISBN 978-0-07-181765-3
e-MHID   0-07-181765-4

Design by Mauna Eichner and Lee Fukui

THIS BOOK SOLELY REFLECTS THE RECOLLECTIONS AND OPIN-IONS OF THE AUTHOR, AND THE AUTHOR IS SOLELY RESPONSI-BLE FOR WHETHER ITS CONTENTS ARE ACCURATE AND TRUE. *THE PATRÓN WAY* IS NOT AFFILIATED WITH, AUTHORIZED BY, OR EN-DORSED BY THE PATRÓN SPIRITS COMPANY OR ANY OF ITS OFFI-CERS, DIRECTORS, SHAREHOLDERS, OR EMPLOYEES.

NEITHER THE ESTATE OF MARTIN CROWLEY NOR WINDSONG TRUST HAS CONTRIBUTED IN ANY WAY TO THE WRITING OF THIS BOOK AND DOES NOT AUTHORIZE OR ENDORSE ITS CONTENTS. NEITHER THE ESTATE OF MARTIN CROWLEY NOR WINDSONG TRUST REP-RESENTS OR WARRANTS THE ACCURACY OR TRUTH OF THE STATE-MENTS, CONVERSATIONS, OR DEPICTIONS CONTAINED HEREIN.

Library of Congress Cataloging-in-Publication Data
Edelstein, Ilana.
  The Patrón way : from fantasty to fortune, lessons on taking any business from idea to iconic brand / by Ilana Edelstein.
     pages cm
   ISBN 978-0-07-181764-6 (alk. paper) — ISBN 0-07-181764-6 (alk. paper)
1. Branding (Marketing) 2. Brand name products. 3. Tequila industry.
  I. Title.
  HF5415.1255.E337 2013
  658.8'27—dc23
                                                                    2013002518

McGraw-Hill Education books are available at special quantity discounts to use as premiums and sales promotions or for use in corporate training programs. To con-tact a representative, please e-mail us at bulksales@mheducation.com.

This book is printed on acid-free paper.

Dedicated to:
Anyone who doesn't have a dream of their own:
follow the one you love and experience
a joyful personal metamorphosis as you help fulfill
his or her passion. It's an extraordinary leap of faith that
could result in the journey of a lifetime.
You'll never know unless you jump in with both feet.

Contents

CONTENTS

Foreword

PATRÓN HAS ACHIEVED iconic status as a brand, with its own celebrated culture and millions of loyal fans in more than 100 different countries. Everyone knows it by name and by its distinctively designed bottle with the world's very best tequila inside. Patrón has been featured in almost 200 hip-hop, rap, country, and pop songs, and is universally celebrated as a symbol of the finest that life has to offer. But until now, some of the story of how it came to be has never been told. Anyone who has ever tried Patrón tequila will be fascinated to learn some of the love, adventure, and turmoil that went into the early creation of this singular spirit. Some even surprised me.

I first met Ilana in 1989, the same year I started Patrón with her life partner, Martin Crowley. Not only did she possess an immense personal charm and beauty, she clearly had a powerful combination of business savvy and creativity. Ilana was already successful in her own business, and her quiet confidence and intelligence added a level of class, sophistication, and credibility to many things in Martin's life.

Ilana was there day and night for so many aspects of this incredible adventure, whether it was creating a celebrity rodeo event that people are talking about to this day, or orchestrating the most unique party the Santa Monica Air Museum has ever seen. Living and breathing the Patrón dream together with Martin, she was so much a part of the Patrón story. Seeing Martin and Ilana in their element together, some might think they could be "Mr. and Mrs. Patrón." Even the way this couple played together was very unique.

Ever the incredible hostess, Ilana came to symbolize the generosity of spirit that is the Patrón lifestyle. Martin and Ilana lived to make every moment memorable. Their home was beautifully decorated, where no detail was too small for their attention, from the party invitations to the exquisitely handblown glasses that served up the vintage wine and tequila.

Their parties were legendary. I should know. My wife, Eloise, and I attended many. We graciously excused ourselves by the time things got too wild, but we always took away with us a feel-good buzz from the amazing food and stimulating conversation, which we enjoyed with Patrón. And we always woke up the next morning feeling great, with the happiest of memories. I will leave it to Ilana to tell you some of the stories about what happened after we left.

Patrón redefined the way people drink tequila. We created a connoisseur's ultrapremium brand in a category where none existed before. It was never about unhealthy excess. It was about celebration. Some of the way Ilana and Martin entertained made you love life and feel more connected to the world. It brought out the best in all of us.

We all contributed in developing and introducing Patrón to the world. Created in Mexico, then headquartered in the Caribbean, and made a world brand, together Martin and I took the business to a level we never imagined possible in those early days. Martin was the creative genius behind Patrón the product and its unique presentation. But, together, Martin and Ilana were part of Patrón's early beating heart.

Ilana did so much for Patrón behind the scenes, from the nuts and bolts of setting up operations in the early days to the creative flourishes of designing the Patrón Girls' costumes; from conceiving major promotional events to training staff and personally answering every e-mail from our customers. She had a way of taking the edge off Martin, enabling him to present his best self. Whether meeting with factory owners or with world leaders with Martin, Ilana was our brand's constant ambassador. Everyone recognized her, and the life she lived was emblematic of Patrón.

Ilana tells her story with grace, compassion, and intelligence. This is no ordinary business memoir. This story is a romance full of drama, intrigue, beauty, and heartbreak. It is unfortunate that Ilana was left out of many things she deserved. Not that she has ever once complained . . . she is so super cool about that.

Throughout these past two decades there have been many, many highs, and a few lows. But there's something in this book for everyone, from devout lovers of our brand to students of our industry, and business in general. You'll come to understand the commitment and passion that go into creating and shaping an authentic brand that's truly an industry game changer. You'll learn about the trailblazers who made it happen. You'll experience it all through the memories and views of Ilana. And while I don't always share in Ilana's memories or views, I'm sure you'll be deeply touched by the selflessness and humanity of this magnificent woman.

This talented lady has produced an enthralling account of the early days of putting together and building a spirits brand from scratch. In this book, you will learn her perspective of how it started and became the world's number one ultrapremium tequila as well as one of the world's most successful brands . . . PATRÓN!

Peace, love, and happiness.

JOHN PAUL DEJORIA
Cofounder, Chairman of the Board,
and a proud owner of Patrón Spirits
International AG

Acknowledgments

John Paul DeJoria (cofounder and owner, Patrón Spirits Co.): Thank you for everything we've shared over the last 24 years — all the fun, encouragement, support, enthusiasm, love, and magic you bring to everything in your sphere. It is a huge endowment to all of us. Thank you, JP, with humility and enormous gratitude.

Dick Weaver (owner, PR Works, my manager): To my oldest friend in America, thank you for that friendship, but equally thank you for all your guidance and understanding. Without you this book would not be possible. Please know that your input was invaluable. Above all, thanks for sticking with me through thick and thin . . . especially the thin!

Jennifer Gates (Zachary Shuster Harmsworth, my literary agent): Thank you for ushering me through this very unfamiliar process with such grace, understanding, and experience, rendering my journey a sheer delight. How lucky I am!

Esmond Harmsworth (Zachary Shuster Harmsworth, also my literary agent): To that beautiful voice and remarkable professionalism and knowledge. Sir, I am so genuinely fortunate to have you on my team. You are the consummate gentleman whose words have a magically calming effect. Thank you.

Samantha Marshall (my collaborator): Thank you for actually "getting" me, and for making this entire experience/process not just painless, but utterly enjoyable. You are one very special and talented lady and I am one very fortunate and happy gal to have had the opportunity and pleasure of working with you.

Mary Glenn, Stacy Ashton, Lydia Rinaldi, Keith Pfeffer, and Pattie Amoroso (the McGraw-Hill team): A huge thank you. I am humbled by our association and in awe of your vast abilities and achievements on my behalf. Each one of you has given me an experience filled with pleasure and harmony, which I will remember fondly forever.

Sharon and Len Ovsiowitz (my sister and brother-in-law): Where do I begin to start thanking you? You are always there for me and, boy, have I inadvertently abused that luxury on occasion! You are my center, my rock, my entire sense of belonging. Thank you for all of it and for giving my life so much meaning with your beautiful and unconditional love and support, not to mention the most wonderful family you have blessed me with. I love you beyond words.

Mark and Rebecca, Gary and Nili Ovsiowitz (my nephews and nieces-in-law): I feel exceptionally fortunate and give thanks every day for having each of you in my life. Thank you for all the joy, fun, and laughter we share, and for always making me such a huge part of your lives. I truly feel important and deeply loved, even though you find me "entertaining." Your interest and attention inspires me daily. I love you with all of my being.

Noah, Caidyn, Casey, and Cole Ovsiowitz (my grandnephew and grandnieces): To the most beautiful and precious four people in my life, you fill me up with pleasure and delight, and I learn from you constantly. Thank heavens for you guys. Please know you can count on me always. I love you so much, my angels. (Noah, remember you need to wait until you're 16 to read this book.)

Nina Svele (the best friend anyone could ever have): Your friendship is one of my most prized possessions. Thank you for being your beautiful self and for *everything* you bring to my life . . . and it's so much! You've been there with me through it all, and I honestly could not have done it without you. Thank you from the bottom of my heart. I love you.

Ted Simpkins, Steve Wallace, Daymond John, Warwick Miller, Caroline and Tom Law, and Gregg Gann: My heartfelt thanks and deepest appreciation for your contributions, not only to these written pages, but for being a part of the amazing rocket ride.

Francisco Alcaraz: Thank you for sharing your warm and gentle beautiful self with us over the years, and for being there every step of the way. Patrón the product has everything to do with you. Your effort, devotion, and friendship are irreplaceable. You will always hold a very tender spot in my heart and I wish you good health and strength for many years to come.

To all the Patrón employees with whom I had the joy of sharing this journey: Burt Stewart, Ed Blinn, Jan Pettaway, Cristy Record, Lynn Hirschberg MacEachern, and all the Patrón girls across the country, it was such a privilege, thank you.

Ron Wong: Thank you for your brilliant graphic designs, past and present. You are a master and both Patrón and I are richer for having worked with you.

All of my clients from I.E. Financial Services and Teachers Financial Services: Thank you for giving me the opportunity to serve you in something I love to do every day.

To the many fans and supporters of the brand, especially the front lines, a huge and embracing hug.

And to Martin: Thank you for the ride of my life!

PART I

R&D

CHAPTER 1

Out of the Blue

MILES OF DUSTY Mexican roads were getting monotonous. The love of my life, Martin Crowley, was just a few days into his monthly buying trip for his new company, Architectural Products Marketing (APM), and was sourcing exquisitely handcrafted tiles, carved stone, marble, ceramics, furnishings, and other architectural pieces from dozens of out-of-the-way factories and quarries in the countryside. The plan was to bring them back to sell to designers and architects building beautiful homes for the millionaires and billionaires living in Beverly Hills and along California's Gold Coast. APM's customers loved his unique and refined taste, and he was doing a roaring trade.

Martin knew exactly where to find the best artisans in Mexico and was an avid collector of objets d'art. He had an eye like no one I'd ever met and the ability to envision how any piece would work in interior and exterior design and landscaping. He was also a brilliant negotiator and could bargain down the price so that the product was practically being given away. But doing that required him to cover a lot of ground, and he was getting exhausted and lonely. To keep himself company, Martin had found a stone carved statue of a *hotei*—a bald, laughing Buddha with a big potbelly. This particular one had a missing toe, and Martin kept him on the car seat next to him. It must have brought him luck.

Whenever he went across the border, he always hired the same driver, Felipe, a local guy who spoke English well and knew the terrain intimately. Martin didn't speak Spanish, and perhaps that was just as well, because when he did speak to anyone Latino, his English suddenly had a Spanish accent. On this particular day of road travel, the pair found themselves in the mountains of Jalisco, about two hours from Guadalajara, smack in the middle of the country.

Lost in the passing landscape, Martin found himself flashing back to a conversation he'd had with his APM business partner and friend, the entrepreneur John Paul DeJoria, earlier that month. Martin and John Paul, or JP, as he is also known, had been drinking shots of Chinaco Tequila when they began speculating about which tequila the aristocrats of Mexico drank. As two men of curiosity and taste, they had this type of conversation regularly. Martin promised to check it out on his next trip to Mexico, and it just so happened that here he was, right in the heart of tequila country.

If he was going to find the finest tequila anywhere, this had to be the place. The highlands overlooking the valley of the Rio Grande provide the perfect conditions for growing blue agave—a plant from the lily family with a core that looks like a giant pineapple, a *pina*. Harvested and processed a certain way, agave is distilled for the production of tequila. But more on that later.

FIELDS OF BLUE

Welcoming a distraction, Martin instructed Felipe to stop at every tequila factory along the way to check out its product. They drove through miles and miles of rolling blue agave fields. God knows how much tequila Martin ended up consuming on this day trip. He lost count. But he was sober enough to remember one extraordinary place.

As soon as he entered the factory, he knew it was different. It was rather small and unusually clean, with wide open spaces and plenty of light and fresh air. Above all, there was a noticeable sense of calm. The property, situated near the highest point of the region, consisted of sparse old adjoining buildings on the side of a hill overlooking a muddy creek. The distillery had been owned by this family for generations, and they still made tequila the old-fashioned way, exactly as they had for 50 years. The place was a complete throwback. The factory had hardly been updated, and apart from a single customer in Japan, their tequila could not be found anywhere outside Mexico.

Its unique flavor was the result of the high-quality agave that was used and the love, method, and care with which it was made. The only ingredient used was premium *Agave tequilana*—Blue Weber agave—and nothing else. At that time, few, if any, factories produced pure agave. Something would always be added to dilute this expensive ingredient, or shortcuts would be adopted in an attempt to replicate the aged flavor, such as adding oak chips in the barrels to quickly create an oak color and flavor.

Martin took one sip of this tequila and knew he didn't need to visit any more factories. Nothing could possibly top this. He bought a few bottles, wrapped up the rest of his buying trip, and headed back to his funky little guest cottage in Hermosa Beach, California.

SPANISH FLY

People assume that Patrón has been around forever, but it was late in the year of 1989 when Martin first discovered what led to this liquid treasure.

By then, we had been together only a few months, but it was one of those once-in-a-lifetime love affairs in which you connect instantly and on every level: physically, spiritually, and intellectually. We'd met in our middle years, already established and leading what we'd assumed were rich and full lives. I was a transplant from my native South Africa, having come to California in the late 1970s to pursue a free-spirited, independent life and live close to my cherished sister and brother-in-law, Sharon and Len. After growing up in a parochial community and chafing under the restrictive rules of apartheid, I relished my newfound freedom in America and saw opportunities to flourish around every corner, eventually building a thriving financial consulting firm.

Martin was a native Californian who'd left his broken home while he was still in his teens, seeking adventure in the Peace Corps, racing his sailing boat around the world, and building a small hotel and restaurants. He was a consummate connoisseur and entrepreneur who could turn any passion into a business. Not only did he flow with endless brilliant ideas, he followed through and actually brought them to life. Possessing more drive and focus than anyone I'd ever met, this was a man with an expansive imagination and the extraordinary ability to turn fantasy into successful tangible reality. Finding our soul mates seemed inconceivable to us, since we had lived our lives without giving it one thought. It was the first time either of us had felt so truly and completely loved, and our world suddenly got bigger, brighter, and better in every way.

We'd met through a mutual friend at a wine tasting. Even in that first flirtatious conversation we had, I learned so much from him about wine. Little did we know at the time that sipping only the very best was to be the beginning of a major theme in our life together.

After that first encounter, we were rarely apart. At this point, we were not yet cohabiting, but we might as well have been. When he wasn't at my place on the Marina Peninsula, I was at his. When he traveled to Mexico, we spoke several times a day. He'd been working so hard to build up his business and recover from a devastating bankruptcy. I'd missed him terribly and couldn't wait to see him again.

When I walked in the door of his beach house, Martin didn't say anything about the tequila, but he had a gleam in his eye. I could tell he had a surprise for me, but there'd be no getting it out of him until he was good and ready. We had our usual reunion: incredible sex, twice; a gourmet meal Martin lovingly prepared; and a bottle of vintage red wine between us. We were relaxed and happy. It was good to have him back.

When I gently teased him for details about his trip, Martin gave me a sly smile, walked over to his still unpacked bag, and pulled out what looked like one of those dusty old decanters a pirate might have taken a swig from 200 years ago.

"Martin, there's a dead fly in the bottle!" I said, pointing to the deceased insect.

"I know. It's Spanish fly, the aphrodisiac," he replied suggestively.

"Really? Let's get it out. I want to try it," I said, knowing full well it was nothing of the kind.

"Forget the fly, honey; you have to taste this tequila," he said, pouring some into a brandy snifter and handing it to me.

"Please, baby, don't ask me to drink tequila. You know the mere smell of the stuff makes me gag."

It was true. As was the case with millions of others, a night of overindulgence in tequila years earlier had made me so sick that I wanted to die; it was the foulest hangover imaginable, and I never wanted to live through it again. I couldn't be anywhere near the stuff without heaving. Besides, hard liquor wasn't my thing; fine wine and champagne were my preference. But Martin's enthusiasm was infectious.

"Come on, hon. I promise you, this tequila is different. You've never tasted anything like it."

"Okay, but I am definitely not downing all of that."

"No, you are not going to shoot it. Just sip it like a fine cognac."

Reluctantly, I put my lips to the glass. What struck me first was the lack of nauseating, gasolinelike tequila fumes. There was a clean and intoxicating aroma to the liquid. I took a tiny sip, and as with fine wine, I let it linger in my mouth for a moment before swallowing.

"Wow!" was all I could say.

For Martin, that was enough. He knew how much I had hated tequila, so I was the perfect control group for this experiment. His discovery had passed the Ilana taste test with flying colors.

A few years later, in an interview with the *Los Angeles Times*, Martin described Patrón as so much more than just a taste; it was an experience: "It's a feeling you get—it's different from drinking vodka or gin. It's more of a psychotropic effect, whether real or imagined."

Martin was able to make his discovery because he was open to what the universe had to offer. His senses were alive, so the moment he tasted the tequila, he understood perfectly the value of what he had found. Many others would have enjoyed a drink, moved on, and forgotten about it, but Martin knew that what he had in his hands was incomparable and that if he felt that way, millions of others would too.

To this day, Patrón is the only spirit I drink, precisely for that reason. Its pure and delicious high cannot be compared to anything else. This is not some high-octane beverage for college kids on spring break. It is so much more refined. No matter how you choose to drink it—mixed as a margarita or sipped straight over ice with lime— you can taste the difference and always experience a cool, smooth finish. The burn that had become synonymous with tequila was gone. Patrón goes down clean and crisp, with no regrets the next morning.

THE GODFATHER

We spent the rest of the evening and the early hours of the morning dreaming up ways this product could be marketed. As design junkies, creating and re-creating was something we loved to do together. Suddenly, we had a new project. Martin came up with the name, Patrón. He wanted a word that meant the same in all the Romance languages. *Patrón* means the good boss or godfather, the guy you go to when you want to marry off your daughter. We liked the aristocratic, dignified way it sounded. The word was easy to pronounce, easy to remember, and portrayed the idea of being the master.

We started modifying and redesigning the bottle. Our prototype was a rather crude and somewhat deformed phallic design with an uneven, elongated neck that was at an angle and a glass stopper. Martin and I were enamored with perfume bottles and packaging and had amassed an extensive assortment between us, so we hauled them out of the bathroom and studied their shapes and labels. We were taking the lead from the fragrance industry, which creates a sense of occasion through exquisite presentation. No one had ever spent that much on packaging in the spirits industry—it almost matched the price of the contents—but as far as we were concerned, it was necessary for the exterior to capture and accurately reflect what was inside. The brand needed a handcrafted look that would suggest that the package's contents were precious and rare. If additional investment was required to create a sense of luxury worthy of Patrón, so be it.

I found a green ribbon and tied it around the bottle's neck while Martin sketched possible labels. He had a little golden honeybee among his hodgepodge of trinkets (which I still have) and came up with the idea of using it as an emblem. Bees are magical creatures. Martin and I consciously tried to be in the moment, so "bee in the moment" wasn't much of a leap. It became one of our marketing taglines for Patrón. Purely as an afterthought, the bee also suggested that the contents of the bottle were irresistible, like nectar.

We knew instinctively that the packaging must creatively, truthfully, and precisely reflect the quality and experience of the contents. For Martin, it wasn't just about marketing; it was his life's philosophy. Years later, looking through some old papers, I came across a handwritten note from Martin that perfectly sums up the significance he gave to beauty in all things:

> *The divine energy put into a true work of art is captured and then radiates back into the environment. The more beauty we surround ourselves with, the more God's creative energy we are exposed to and can metabolize into our own being and synergistically grow with the beautiful and loving energy.*

He then signed it with a phrase he used repeatedly: "Truth and beauty are lovers."

Martin knew that design is so much more than just a look. It also has the power to create a powerful emotion in the consumer. It's an approach that makes the difference between iconic consumer brands such as Coke, Chanel No. 5, even Campbell's Soup and just another product that gets lost in the crowd.

Once we were on a roll, there was no stopping us. We were both guilty of succumbing to designer's disease. At one point, after hours of tinkering, we sat back and looked at the little bottle, and Martin turned to me, sighed wistfully, and said, "Wouldn't it be wild if this became the top-selling tequila in the world?"

The only problem was that neither of us knew a thing about the liquor industry.

NOTHING VENTURED . . .

The next night, we went to dinner at John Paul DeJoria's house in Beverly Hills. People know JP mainly as the owner of John Paul Mitchell Systems. He's the handsome, swarthy guy with the beard and ponytail featured in all the magazine ads, along with his exquisite wife, Eloise, a blonde Texan beauty. But what many people may not realize is that John Paul is a savvy investor with a hand in multiple business and philanthropic ventures. It's as if he has some sort of sixth sense about what will succeed, and almost everything he touches turns to platinum.

In John Paul's words, he was the "bank" in his partnership with Martin. This successful business marriage led to a friendship among the four of us, so we were often at one another's homes dining or partying. One of the few conditions JP asked of Martin was that whatever they did together should always be fun. He understood perfectly that a brand is only as good as the quality of the people involved. He shared our deeply held belief that what separates a good product from a great one are the intangible but powerful forces of the human spirit. For this and many other reasons, I adore John Paul and Eloise.

Martin brought the mocked-up bottle of tequila to dinner with us, with the fly removed of course, and poured John Paul a shot in a brandy snifter.

"Here it is, JP, the finest tequila in Mexico, and I believe with the help of tequila master Francisco Alcaraz, it can be made even better. I don't know what tequila the aristocrats drink now, but I do know what they'll be drinking in the near future."

"Wow. Martin, you're right; this is it!" exclaimed John Paul. "We're partners. Go back to Mexico, get Francisco involved, and buy a thousand cases. Worst case, if it doesn't sell, we'll have the world's best tequila for ourselves and our friends and family."

A DEAL THEY COULDN'T REFUSE

Soon afterward, Martin went back to the factory with Felipe and made the owners an offer. He would make a commitment to their entire production, providing all the bottling and packaging materials, but they couldn't sell to anyone else. We hadn't sold a dime's worth of tequila yet; his goal was to tie up the source. The family owners agreed to his terms. They must have thought Martin was a complete madman, but who would say no to a 100 percent guarantee of sales?

Back in Hermosa Beach, we continued designing. Martin and I bounced more ideas off each other in a creative frenzy, feeding off each other's imaginations as we took one concept and then raised the bar to the next level and the next. We were literally consumed with creating something that would do justice to this superb product. Like proud parents, we pampered and reveled in our newborn. Our efforts were truly joint and completely intertwined; enhancing our baby was our singular goal. There was no competing or even differentiating; we were just two impassioned beings, trusting their intent and creativity and surrendering to everything in the process. As much as we recognized each other's imprint on our progeny, we thrilled and marveled at what the magical mixture of our creative DNA had brought to life.

Little by little, our packaging evolved into the ultrapremium gift look you see on the shelves today. By then, with the help of Ron Wong, a stellar graphic designer and friend, we'd already designed the labels, with wording, ribbons, a booklet, tissue paper, and a box. Ron also created a usable mock-up of the bottle for us. Fortunately, Martin was able to use his sourcing expertise to find Cesar Hernandez, owner of the only remaining glassblowing factory in Mexico where they still used artisans to handblow each bottle. Perfecting our bottle design was a lengthy process of trial and error. The bottles were made from 100 percent recycled glass, not too dissimilar from the original hive-shaped bottle, with glass stoppers, like true decanters. Later, Martin added the punt at the bottom, as on wine bottles, and had the word *Patrón* embossed in the glass on the side.

It was an attention to detail that simply was not done in those days. The liquor giants spent staggering amounts of money developing a new product. They hired "teams" of experts and consultants from every avenue, who essentially "constructed" a product on the basis of their evaluation and interpretation of analyses, statistics, feasibilities, trends, and so on. Charts are used and probabilities are applied, but unfortunately, no amount of time, money, research, or labor will produce a product that possesses soul, personality, a true identity, or any of the essential elements that captivate. Those are intangibles that cannot be bought, manufactured, manipulated, or even faked; they seem to evolve purely organically when intention and desire, honesty and humility, humor and creativity, and passion and fun are all present, balanced, and in harmony.

The same giants sank millions into print and billboard ads that left no lasting impression. One notable exception was Absolut Vodka, which had incorporated art into its bottle design, initially commissioning Andy Warhol in 1986 to create the first of many decorated bottle "collections." This campaign reflected the premium quality of the vodka, which was its own boutique brand in a market that had long been dominated by corporate brands. Although Martin and I were aware of Absolut's campaign at the time and admired some of its more clever and beautiful pieces, we were content to operate in our own creative bubble, making sure we didn't miss a thing in our painstaking bottle and package design.

Friends who came to dine at Martin's beach cottage could not get over the number of Patrón bottle prototypes we had lining the windowsills and covering just about every flat surface. They oohed and aahed over the design flourishes, and we made a mental note of every single reaction. I wrapped a neon green ribbon around the necks of our favorites, and we edited the selection down until our final design matched our exacting taste and standards, incorporating all the elements we knew our discerning customers might appreciate. During those earliest Patrón parties, our home was our design lab, and we had our very own group of market survey participants who were delighted to give us their feedback.

Next, Martin began the process of trademarking the name and, later, the bottle design—the second trademark ever issued for a bottle design, after Coke. It was an ingenious act of incredible prescience. We also shopped, researched, and procured sources for the labels, the boxes, the ribbons, and every other accoutrement that would elevate this product above everything else that was currently on the market. Martin spent hours on the phone with the makers of those products, first ensuring top quality and then squeezing the price down as far as he could. With so many items sourced from different corners of the world, we began to realize that every penny counted.

It was the first half of 1990, and sales of our first shipment were slow, but momentum gradually started to build. We were at the start of a bad recession, and no one had ever paid $47 for a bottle of tequila. People laughed. They couldn't decide if we were being audacious or insane. No one had ever seen tequila presented in this manner. They definitely hadn't tasted anything like it before. This was top shelf. Martin used to say, "People would always find money for their indulgences, no matter what the cost." We were in our own bubble. We didn't have any competitors. No one was doing anything like this, so we weren't looking over our shoulders; we were simply following our own best instincts.

BACK TO BASICS

Tequila has been around since the Spanish conquered Mexico, but it had long since been cheapened by mass market producers. By keeping it pure and using only the finest blue agave, we were simply going back to the basics, making Patrón the way tequila was produced by the conquistadores. We envisioned that Patrón would be marketed much the way a fine cognac or single malt whiskey was sold—to connoisseurs with a discerning palate.

Not knowing where to start, we chose the route that made the most sense to us, romancing and educating what we called the front line: bartenders and club and restaurant owners. Everywhere we went, Martin would carry a bottle of Patrón with us. On a typical evening, we'd walk into a Los Angeles–area restaurant, usually around 5 p.m., before it got busy, and take our place at the bar. We would show the bartender our bottle and ask for two glasses. Martin would pour a shot of Patrón into one glass and invite the bartender to pour a shot of whatever he considered the finest tequila on his shelf into the other glass, which we would pay for. He would then instruct the unsuspecting bartender to sip the tequila, not shoot it. No matter what other tequila was chosen, the immediate response after tasting both was always the same: "Wow!" It never failed.

We did this hundreds of times. Educating the bar staff became our top priority. Tequila had always been a spirit that was consumed to get drunk; it was never considered a refined, exquisite-tasting elixir. We realized we had to reverse an entire population's perception of tequila. It was all about legwork, personal interaction, and pure gut instinct. With those results, it wasn't difficult to arrange on-premise promotions. This is how Patrón was introduced to the world. The odds were stacked against us as no one had ever paid that much for tequila before, much less sipped it. Then again, neither had anyone met the owner of a brand like this.

We eventually got to know the owners and staff of countless bars, restaurants, and liquor stores throughout the Los Angeles area. We arranged for "Patrón Nights," hosting prix fixe dinners that paired dishes with Patrón-based cocktails. These events took place at least a decade before it was commonplace to do tastings and pairings with spirit brands. If anything, this was done only for fine vintage wine tastings.

One of our early adopters, in 1991, was Lula Cocina Mexicana on Main Street in Santa Monica, one of the more popular Mexican places and still a major establishment in that trendy shopping and dining district. We took over a portion of the restaurant and offered a set menu that included a margarita before dinner, Patrón Silver served ice cold and straight up with lime to accompany ceviche scallops, Patrón Anejo to go with mole chicken, and Patrón XO Cafe, our coffee-flavored tequila, to complement a rich crème brûlée.

Martin and I were there to meet, greet, and eat with the 30 discerning diners who packed the event. Lula was thrilled because it brought more customers to her restaurant, and we were happy because it enabled us to introduce our brand in a controlled setting that conveyed the idea that Patrón was a gourmet's spirit meant to be sipped as an aperitif or digestif and to accompany a great meal in the same manner as a fine Bordeaux. The event was so successful that Lula had us back every couple of months and arranged for similar events to take place in the half dozen other restaurants she owned in the area.

But our up-close and personal approach wasn't just for the bars and restaurants. Martin also focused on building a relationship with retailers throughout Los Angeles. We became friends with about a dozen liquor and specialty store owners, socializing and dining with them and receiving their special attention in return. Even though their spaces were relatively small, Martin persuaded them to put in floor stacks of Patrón: cases of product piled high on the aisle floor to grab the attention of shoppers. The practice is usually limited to supermarkets, which have extra space, so by doing this in the smaller shops we made our brand really stand out. Although we never discounted Patrón, we'd often include some swag with the purchases.

One local retailer, Steve Wallace of Wally's Wine & Spirits, was and is well known in LA for putting together a year-end catalog of fabulous arrangements with gourmet treats, vintage wines, champagnes, and spirits. Steve included us in the arrangements, which was perfect because it directly associated us with only the most high-end products and put in consumers' minds the idea that drinking Patrón was an occasion.

All these relationships helped. We were getting people hooked and creating a following. We helped the front lines of retail establishments, restaurants, and bars create buzz with events and promotions, and they in turn became our best marketers.

With so many boots on the ground, word soon spread about this amazing new tequila. There's nothing like true passion and conviction when you're selling a product. Our enthusiasm for Patrón went viral across Southern California the old-fashioned way: word of mouth. Friends of Patrón genuinely loved this brand. It became the only thing they would drink.

THE STANDOUT

While Martin and I were promoting Patrón to restaurant and bar owners, John Paul was using every opportunity to introduce it in celebrity circles, and he never went out without a bottle in each hand.

Martin was incredibly fortunate to have JP as his partner. It was through him that Patrón landed its first distributor, Wine Warehouse, based in Southern California. They were small and regional, but the advantage was that until then they carried wine exclusively, so this was the first and only spirit on their books. Rather than being buried among 50 other brands of spirit, Patrón stood out. Turns out, it's exactly what was needed in those early days.

JP's contacts and our own work in the trenches all helped tremendously. There was an undercurrent building in Los Angeles, and the buzz had made Patrón something of a scarce commodity. Within a few short months we ran out of our first shipment. This test run showed us that we could afford to scale up and order as much Patrón as the factory could produce. However, what we did not anticipate was how quickly demand would exceed supply. For an upstart, it was both an enviable and a potentially fatal position to be in. Blindly, we wanted to cover more ground, getting our bottles into stores and bars across the country. No one could have foreseen this predicament, and there was no one to show us the way. Who knew our factory's maximum production capacity would become inadequate so soon? But that was part of the magic. By not knowing how things were supposed to be done or allowing for a little forecasting, we inadvertently turned traditional business practice on its head and figured out a better way.

Sometimes ignorance really is bliss. Of course it's important to know the basics of business, but that doesn't mean you must always go by the book. Don't be afraid to set your own bar. Winners don't limit themselves by an industry's norm. The only way to truly be a breakout success is to block out the noise and listen to your own best instincts.

VEGAS, BABY

Never did this clever cluelessness serve us better than on our first trip to Las Vegas.

We went there on a mission, Martin and I. Our goal was to find a hot girl. Not just any kind of hot. She had to have everything: elegance, a winning smile, a lovely face, a perfect arse, and huge, firm boobs. If they were fake, even better. She couldn't be trashy; men and women alike had to look at her with lust.

No, we weren't scouting for a partner in a threesome, not that I was entirely against the idea. This was strictly business. It was 1990, and we were offered a booth that had just become available at the annual Wine and Spirits Wholesalers of America (WSWA) convention, the biggest liquor industry trade show in the country and our first convention ever. We assumed that alcohol would be presented much the same way cars were at auto shows, with tantalizing half-dressed women draped all over the place. We needed a gorgeous Patrón Girl to lure foot traffic to our booth and get people to notice us and taste our tequila, because it was only by experiencing Patrón that they could fully appreciate the fact that this was a brand like no other in the world.

Martin got the call only two days before the show was starting, so we had to kick into gear. My first thought was to hire a Patrón Girl and dress her in a classy but sexy outfit. We had some T-shirts emblazoned with "Team Patrón" lying around that I cut up and had my tailor apply onto two tight black Lycra minidresses that were hanging in my closet. The outfits showed every curve and needed to be complemented by the perfect body.

BOOBS OR BUST

The night before the convention, we met an agent in Las Vegas who took us to every hotel and casino that had show girls: MGM Grand, Caesar's Palace, the Riviera, Bally's. . . . We went from venue to venue when we knew the girls would be on break, interviewing dozens of stunners and having them try on the Patrón outfit. They had legs that went on forever and not an ounce of flab on them. There was just one problem: no boobs. These dancing girls were lithe and beautiful, but they had bodies like teenage boys. It simply wasn't going to work with the dress I'd designed, because the tightness of the Lycra was squashing down what little they had in the chest region and making them flat as pancakes.

By now it was 4 a.m., the agent had long since gone home, and we still didn't have our girl. We were starting to worry. How on earth were we going to make an impact with all these established brands without some bait? Martin and I didn't need to say a word. We were both thinking the same thought: This is Vegas, baby!

There were sexy young things all over the place, and their work shift had only just begun. I grabbed the Yellow Pages, called an escort agency—Desert Foxes—and started interviewing hookers. I could just imagine the expression of the madam on the other end of the line.

"We need a girl to work a convention tomorrow," I explained.

"Oh, yeah? Sure, no problem," she replied, snickering.

"We need her to come over now to try on an outfit to make sure it works."

"Hmmmmm. . . . What kind of weird stuff are you into?"

"I'm being serious; it's for a convention," I persisted. "Send me only your most refined-looking girls and please make sure they have boobs."

We began interviewing a parade of prostitutes. Some of them were leery of us and came with beefy-looking guys, probably strip club bouncers, for protection. I completely understood. They had no idea what they were walking into. A few of them were sweet and attractive, but under the harsh lighting they'd be exposed to at the liquor show, they had a kind of hardness about them. It just wouldn't do.

WORKING GIRL

Finally, we met Sammy, the only girl brave enough to come see us on her own. She was a knockout and filled out that dress to perfection. You would never guess her profession. She had it all: class, a naturally seductive beauty, a charming personality, and a spectacular pair of breasts.

Later that morning, Sammy showed up at our booth precisely on time. She was thrilled to be doing something to put food on the table for her two young kids besides turning tricks. I liked her even more in the cold light of day. Though no paragon of virtue myself, I couldn't imagine doing what she did to earn a living, but I was fascinated to learn more about her and the world she came from. She was just doing what was necessary to survive.

Running on reserve energy, I took her into the ladies' room and dressed her. Then I got myself ready, as the two of us would be working the booth together. We carried those dresses beautifully, and the Patrón bee was framed in a green heart emblazoned on our backsides. Well, let's just say they proved to be an enticing invitation to bee in love with the brand.

Everything about our booth was different from the rest. It was right at the entrance, so it would be the first one that visitors would see. We covered our space in the Patrón colors—green, black, mango, and silver—and stocked up with lots of finely made swag to give away. We draped our sampling table in black silk, laying it with fine crystal glasses and beautiful hammered silver vases filled with Casablanca lilies. It was feminine and elegant next to the predictable Bristol board signage and bland displays and presentations of our trade counterparts. In a male-dominated industry, we certainly stood out. But I suspect that's not what drew all those men to our stand. In less than an hour, we were 20 deep with potential buyers eager to flirt with two buxom blondes and have a taste of something new.

ABOUT LAST NIGHT

By day 2, word had spread about our booth, and the crowd grew so big that it blocked the entrance to the convention. We were giddy with excitement over the way Patrón had stolen the entire show. All of a sudden Sammy pulled me behind the curtain at the back of the booth. She looked horrified.

"What's wrong, luv?" I asked.

"Oh, Ilana, I don't know how to tell you this, but do you see those two men out there?"

I peeked out and saw two nondescript, balding middle-aged guys in suits.

"Yes. What about them?"

"I was with them last night. The two of them—they were taking turns with me. You wouldn't believe what they were into. And now they're going to recognize me. I'm so sorry. What do you want me to do?"

"Nothing, Sam. Trust me, they're not going to say anything. They're married men; I can see their wedding rings, so they will be more than grateful not to be acknowledged. Just be your usual friendly self and pretend you've never met before. Believe me, it's not your problem, it's theirs."

The poor girl was practically in tears. She didn't want anything to jeopardize her new gig. I did my best not to laugh, but the whole situation struck me as absurd. So many of these guys used the trade show as an excuse to party. This was a junket for them, and apparently they took the saying "What happens in Vegas stays in Vegas" quite literally.

We hired Sammy for events several times after that. On one occasion, we even flew her to Los Angeles. She was that good, and people loved her. She was the first Patrón Girl, and Patrón soon became known for the gorgeous and well-informed young ladies who represented the brand. They had to be polished, personable, and as passionate about Patrón as we were. We found them everywhere: waitressing in restaurants, walking along the street, hanging out in bars, training horses, even working in strip clubs. But they all had one thing—or I should say two things—in common.

As incredible as it seems, we were the only exhibitor with girls; no one else had them. We were the talk of the trade show, and before long the entire industry was buzzing about what we'd done. Suddenly, Patrón Tequila was the brand on everyone's lips. The next year, everyone had girls working at the conventions.

But it was clear they had missed the point. Liquor marketing still consisted of middle-aged men in suits with rather ordinary cardboard branding. It wasn't just our girls; our entire presentation was sexy, right down to the display table covering. What the rest of the industry also failed to understand was that by just having attractive girls and no message, they were selling only sex. It got your attention, but once they had it, they didn't do anything with it. It was a huge lost opportunity. No one had educated their girls, therefore no product information or titillation was being disseminated. But the Patrón Girls weren't just delicious eye candy; they were true brand ambassadors, using their looks and cheeky good humor to attract customers' attention and then surprise and dazzle them with their encyclopedic and intimate knowledge of the brand.

As complete newbies to the industry, it never occurred to us to do anything else. Having stunning young women promoting our brand, creating an atmosphere of sophistication, beauty, conviviality, and excitement around our tequila, just seemed obvious. After all, cocktailing is supposed to be about being social and having a fabulous time. At least it is with our brand.

Finally, we'd put Patrón on the national map. From an obscure, dusty factory high up in the hills of central Mexico, our tequila was now on the lips of every tastemaker in the land.

We were true game changers. Now all we had to do was deliver.

CHAPTER 2

A Brief History
of Tequila

GREAT BRANDS aren't just born from a vacuum. Understanding their rich history and context only serves to enrich the experience of producing, selling, and consuming an iconic product such as Patrón.

We knew precious little about the origins of tequila before Martin encountered Patrón, but we quickly realized that Francisco Alcaraz, our master distiller at the Jalisco factory and one of the foremost experts on tequila in the world, was a treasure trove of information about a beverage with roots as ancient and mysterious as the Aztecs.

As it happens, tequila is the perfect blend of Old World and New World cultures. Over the course of many dinners at our home in California, Francisco described how hundreds of years before the Spanish arrived in the sixteenth century, the Tiquila tribe from Amatitlan in present-day Guatemala learned the process of boiling and fermenting the agave plant to obtain a ritualistic beverage that was consumed only by religious authorities. In other words, only gods and priests were deemed fit to drink this precursor of tequila.

I was charmed to learn that there is even an Aztec goddess associated with what became the basis of tequila: Mayahuel. A stunning beauty blessed with 400 breasts to feed her 400 children, she defied her celestial family to run away with Quetzalcoatl, the god of redemption. The two hid from her wicked grandmother by turning themselves into the branches of a leafy tree, but she found them and ordered the execution of the newlyweds.

Quetzalcoatl, the husband, somehow survived, but Mayahuel was shredded into tiny pieces by the stars. Quetzalcoatl buried her remains in the earth, from which sprouted the first crop of agave plants. The gods in their continued fury struck down the plants with a lightning bolt. The enormous plant caught fire, and when its spiny leaves were consumed by the flames, leaving only the heart, or *pina*, behind, it oozed with the blood of Mayahuel, an intoxicating and aromatic nectar as sweet as honey that captivated all who came near it.[1] This is the origin of its role in Aztec culture as a ceremonial offering to the gods.

Delving further into the history and origins of tequila for the writing of this book, I was amazed at the goldmine of information that is out there. From almost nothing when we first began our journey with Patrón, there are now entire websites dedicated to tequila, and aficionados who do nothing but blog about the beverage. I've included some of the most fascinating details here, with web references for those who wish to investigate further. As for our goddess, there is more:

It is said that Mayahuel, who is also the Mexican goddess of alcohol, came upon the idea of fermenting the agave by observing a drunken mouse drink agave juice.[2] The resulting magical concoction, which Mexican Indians called octli, later become known as pulque, a vitamin-rich brew widely considered to be the early ancestor of mezcal.

Agave played a huge role in early Latin American society, and not only for its nutritional properties. Evidence of its use has been found in prehistoric burial sites and dates back to 7000 BC. The plant's leaves produced fiber that was used for clothing, rope, and other household items. For this and many other reasons, the plant was named *el Arbol de las Maravillas*, or "the Tree of Marvels," according to a 1596 history of Central America.[3]

MYTH BUSTING

Such uniquely Latin lore surrounds tequila and the story of its origins, although not all myths are that poetic. Perhaps the most widespread misconception is that tequila contains a worm in the bottle. In fact, great tequila never has anything but great tequila in the bottle. This urban legend was perpetrated in the 1940s by some American brands that put worms in their bottles as part of a cheap marketing ploy to boost sales. Somehow, people got the idea that when consumed, these insects have special hallucinogenic or psychotropic properties. If only that were true!

Some believe the worm myth derived from a caterpillar infestation that affected some of the agave plants used in the production of mezcal. Apparently, one is supposed to eat the worm or, more accurately, the larva, in the mezcal.[4] The larvae are safe to consume, although I can't imagine why anyone would want to. But they are a feature of some brands of mezcal only, not of tequila.

APPLES TO ORANGES

Exactly when tequila reached its present form remains a matter of debate. People often confuse tequila with mezcal wine or mezcal brandy, which is said by some to be the grandfather of tequila. But they are most definitely not the same thing. The type of agave, the region where it is grown, and the production and process are completely different, as is the taste. Mezcal, which is generally rough and burns the throat on its way down, is to an ultrapremium tequila such as Patrón what cheap rye is to a fine single-malt whiskey. The basic ingredient is similar, but the results are night and day. Mezcal has become more popular among mixologists of late. I can only imagine that's because success breeds success. Tequila's "grandfather," or rather its poor third cousin, is riding the wave of the global tequila craze.

Mezcal is made from different varieties of the agave plant (there are 136 species in Mexico) grown mostly in the state of Oaxaca, but tequila is only made from Blue Weber agave, a far superior plant that is grown exclusively in Jalisco and a handful of surrounding states. The traditional way of making mezcal involves scraping out the sugary heart of the agave and baking it in a rock-covered pit over charcoal to produce a strong, smoky flavor, whereas *pinas* destined to make tequila are baked in aboveground ovens. There are many other distinctions related to the harvesting and processing of the agave as well as the fact that mezcal is distilled only once, whereas proper tequila is distilled at least two or three times.[5]

MOTHER OF INVENTION

Mezcal wine had been fermented but not actually distilled into something stronger until around 1520, when necessity became the mother of invention for those hard-drinking Spaniards who had landed in the New World. Although no one is sure when a Spanish colonist first came across the native drink, it is believed that when the early conquistadores ran out of their own supplies of brandy, they introduced

Moorish methods of distillation to this agave extraction, producing North America's first distilled spirit. Or at least that is one version of how the distillation process was introduced. Another theory has it that Filipino sailors on Spanish galleons from Manila introduced distillation to the natives when they docked at Jalisco. They brought their stills to make coconut brandy, and the Mexican Indians adapted them to start their own cottage industry of mezcal production.[6]

Some 80 years later, around 1600, legend has it that the man known as the Father of Tequila, Don Pedro Sánchez de Tagle, the marquis of Altamira, began mass-producing tequila at the first factory in the territory of modern-day Jalisco. King Philip II of Spain had earlier banned the planting of vineyards in Mexico to eliminate competition with Spanish products in the New World, so Don Pedro saw an opportunity, taking advantage of the blue agave plants native to the region that had until then been something of an afterthought for Spanish traders. They tended to prefer rum. It was going to be a hard sell, but this visionary Spanish noble was not deterred. He built the largest hacienda in the region, launched the import-export trade in what was still technically mezcal wine, and acquired a huge fortune. Of course, the facts of this story cannot be confirmed and are still in dispute.[7]

HEALING PROPERTIES

Having a plentiful supply of an alcoholic beverage was essential to the survival of the colonists, who were accustomed to drinking wine or beer with their meals. It wasn't wise to drink the water in Mexico any more than it was safe in Europe. The alcohol also helped kill any bacteria lingering from less than sanitary food preparation. The early variations of tequila not only served this purpose, they also were considered to have medicinal properties. Spanish doctors even used it as a balm externally to treat conditions such as rheumatism.[8]

Although some of these stories about tequila's early origins are up for debate, we do know for certain that the village of Tequila was officially founded in 1656. The region of Jalisco, originally called New Galicia, was in the outer reaches of the colony and was inhabited by natives who were among the toughest for the conquistadores to conquer, and it's doubtful it would have held much interest for the Spanish if not for the discovery of its richest resource, the blue agave. Tequila itself, situated 34 miles northeast of Guadalajara, rests on an extinct volcano that rises nearly 10,000 feet above sea level. Its arid, steep terrain with reddish clay for soil provides ideal conditions for growing blue agave, albeit little else. Today the town of Tequila, internationally known for its main industry, remains something of an outback, with a population of just 30,000.

MASS PRODUCTION

In 1758, Spain began granting land specifically for the cultivation of agave in Mexico, and Jose Cuervo, a Spanish entrepreneur, was given rights over a vast territory in Jalisco.[9] By the middle of the next century, his family business came to own more than 3 million agave plants. By 1880, Cuervo was selling 10,000 barrels a year.[10]

Several other large and small producers soon followed suit, including the precursors of the present-day brands Tequila Herradura and La Perseverancia Sauza. But it wasn't until after 1821, after Mexico gained independence and Mexicans no longer had easy access to Spanish imports, that tequila gained any significance to the national economy. Agricultural methods became more organized, production methods advanced, and industrial kilns known as autoclaves were introduced to replace the traditional conical holes dug in the ground, enabling faster boiling.

The introduction of a rail system in Mexico allowed tequila to be shipped to farther-flung regions, and soon the spirit caught the attention of the tax authorities, which imposed levies to raise revenues to help fund the Mexican revolution and the fight against the continued presence of the emperor Maximilian. Over the next few decades, because of its association with independence and the revolution, Mexicans developed a deep national pride in tequila, which replaced French products such as cognac as the preferred spirit.

In the late nineteenth century, Don Cenobio Sauza, municipal president of the village of Tequila, became the first to export tequila to the United States, a total of eight barrels. Don Cenobio's grandson, Don Francisco Javier, led the push for higher production standards, gaining international attention for reportedly insisting that "there cannot be tequila where there are no agaves."[11] In 1873 the beverage produced in the region was officially designated tequila to distinguish it from mezcal. The rules for tequila became even stricter in 1944, when the Mexican government determined that only products made through the distillation of agave in the state of Jalisco could be labeled tequila.

Today, almost all of the country's tequila producers exist within a 100-mile radius of Tequila, and the number of factories has exploded since we launched the first ultrapremium brand. As of 2012, there were 144 registered tequila distilleries producing 1,269 brands, with companies ranging from tiny family-owned *fábricas* to huge plants with state-of-the-art technology.[12] Thus, Patrón truly did come from the original source. Our own brand of tequila was and still is as authentic as you can get.

BOOM TO BUST
TO BOOM

The rest of the story of tequila is a series of boom and bust cycles. An outbreak of Spanish influenza in northern Mexico helped solidify its popularity among Mexican consumers when doctors prescribed a shot of tequila with lemon and salt to treat the illness, a tradition that has continued, although most definitely not for medicinal purposes.[13] Sales also rose in the United States during World War II, when European spirits weren't easily available. Tequila was much closer to home, and so many Americans who had never tasted the beverage before became accustomed to it. But tequila sales collapsed again in the mid-1950s, when competition returned and peacetime regulations made it harder for Mexican distillers to export.

Meanwhile, as distillers modernized production and farming techniques, the Mexican authorities began to further tighten their rules for the tequila industry. In 1947, it was decreed that tequila had to be made from at least 51 percent blue agave. In 1959, the Camara Regional de la Industria Tequilera, Mexico's official tequila board, was formed, and authorities based in Guadalajara began taking its role in safeguarding the integrity of the industry much more seriously. They became increasingly savvy about the national and international markets, continually raising the standards that allow a spirit to bear the hallowed name *tequila*. It was a matter of national pride as well as good business practice.

Sales, along with production, continued to rise steadily from the 1960s onward, although an economic slump and the severe Mexican economic crisis of the early 1980s once more resulted in a decline. For several years in the late 1990s, a severe agave shortage continued to hobble growth. More on this later.

TRAILBLAZER

But this was just the calm before an explosion of popularity. Before Patrón came along, tequila had long been a bit player in the spirits market, with domestic consumption hovering at a mere 6 million nine-liter cases in 1997, compared with 32.9 million cases for vodka. The market was and still is dominated by vodka and to some extent rum, although it varied according to region, with Scotch drinkers in New York, Bourbon drinkers in the South and Midwest, and almost all tequila sales restricted to the Southwest. But Patrón and the premiumization movement it ignited changed all that, with a more diverse consumer base demanding high quality. Today, we have legions of imitators in all spirit categories. Even some Bourbon brands, once imbibed only in the bars of the Deep South, have followed the path we carved out for them by launching ultrapremium small-batch products such as Buffalo Trace and Woodford Reserve, aged, distilled, and filtered multiple times and inventively packed with that handcrafted look. Over the last two decades, the liquor industry has transformed itself, and more sophisticated palates seek out only the best.

Patrón itself started out selling only about 10,000 cases a year. As of 2011, Patron had sold close to 2 million cases, becoming the world's largest tequila brand in terms of retail sales at $1.1 billion.[14] As of 2010, overall sales of tequila were estimated at 11.6 million cases, with Americans drinking record amounts, according to the latest statistics by the Mexican tequila board. And it's partly because Patrón led the charge and created a whole new category: ultrapremium tequila. Sales of tequila priced at more than $22 a bottle have grown by 317 percent since 2003, according to DISCUS, the Distilled Spirits Council of the United States.[15]

Today, the market is in oversupply and the dynamic caused by the agave shortage is in reverse. More and more 100 percent agave products are coming to market, and Patrón has legions of imitators, including, I believe, one that was launched through the hit HBO series *Entourage*. There are now over 100 distilleries making over 900 brands of tequila in Mexico, and over 2,000 brand names have been registered. This is helping to raise quality perceptions overall, and in turn demand is surging not only in core Mexican and U.S. markets but across a number of countries.

Patrón maintains its position as the leader of the connoisseur market of aged and ultrapremium tequilas to sip and savor like fine cognac despite the proliferation of new brands. The outlook for the category Patrón helped create has never been better. Now a mature and established spirit category, tequila is entering a stage of consolidation in world markets. It is no longer a fad. The fact that 100 percent agave tequila exports have increased tremendously over the last two years suggests that tequila sales, particularly premium and ultrapremium brands, have entered a whole new phase of popularity since tequila was discovered by the Spanish conquerors all those centuries ago.

CHAPTER 3

The Taste Test

I T WAS EITHER going to make us or kill us. Martin had decided to throw caution to the wind and publicly challenge the top-selling tequilas on the market to a blind taste test, hoping to build instant brand awareness among the consuming public. It was a risky move indeed. If Patrón failed to make the grade, it would be free and fabulous advertising for the other guy and would absolutely ruin us.

Wolfgang Puck, a friend of John Paul's, gave us the ideal venue: Spago, the hot spot where all the movers and shakers at the time did lunch. Only this was more of a liquid lunch. The mere fact that we were doing a tequila-fueled event in the middle of the day on a Thursday was enough to generate extraordinary buzz. This was 1991, when the three-martini lunches of the roaring 1980s were a thing of the past and the idea of having such an elaborate event in the midst of economic hardship caused by the ongoing recession was unthinkable. That, plus the sheer ballsiness of what we were trying to prove, had everyone in Tinseltown talking.

My dear friend Dick Weaver, a former colleague from my PR days who now had his own boutique publicity firm, PR Works, was hired for the launch. He represented an interesting array of clients across a broad spectrum of industries and had a unique approach to public relations. Dick brought together a panel of distinguished judges, including his client Luis Barajas, founder and editor of *Detour*, the hippest magazine in Los Angeles at the time, as well as famed Hollywood columnist and socialite Joan Quinn. We also had several top food and beverage critics and restaurateurs, including the well-known Los Angeles tastemaker Steve Wallace, owner of the luxury retailer Wally's, so our judges were highly respected and had serious clout. For added authenticity, we hired Ernst & Young to overlook and tally the results, just as they do at the Oscars.

And of course there were celebrities. Dick happened to be on the board of Earth Communications Office (ECO), the first environmental organization to raise awareness about global warming. He convinced Martin and JP that rather than try to get celebrities to the event one by one, they should make a sizable donation to ECO through Patrón. Following that advice, they gave $10,000 to the cause and encouraged ECO's participation. ECO in turn invited its major players to attend, maximizing the PR benefit. It was one-stop shopping.

Among the luminaries on the A-list board were Tom Cruise, Mimi Rogers (the first Mrs. Tom Cruise), Arnold Schwarzenegger, Ed Begley Jr., Esai Morales, Sara Gilbert, and the Olympic gold medalist and AIDS activist Greg Louganis, some of whom attended the event. Other stars on the scene included James Coburn, a friend of JP's, and Lara Flynn Boyle, Dick's dear friend. It was to be more like a movie premiere than a product launch.

Every detail had to be perfect, because this was Patrón's first extensively media-covered event. I had beautifully embossed invitations made in black with the Patrón colors, tied with green ribbon. We had our glassblowing factory in Mexico send us 150 custom-made half-size Patrón bottles as swag for our guests, but when they arrived from the factory the day before the event, they were covered in sawdust and needed to be washed, dressed with labels and ribbons, and filled with Patrón. Luckily, we had some free labor on hand in the form of my 11- and 13-year-old nephews, Gary and Mark, our chief bottle washers, working at night in our Marina del Rey home. Their nimble little fingers were just what we needed to affix the half-size labels, and they were thrilled to be involved.

No, we weren't leaving minors unattended while they bottled 80-proof alcohol. Our girlfriend Deborah Herman was on hand to help and supervise. Leaving the three of them alone, we entertained our guests of honor, the family member owners managing the factory, as well as Francisco, our master tequila blender, whom we had flown in from Jalisco for the event. Apart from Francisco, they spoke little, if any, English, so we invited Simon Winthrop, a magician we'd met in Marina del Rey, to perform tricks and keep them amused at dinner. When Martin and I first saw Simon, we were entranced by his beautiful smiling face and spirit. We knew we had to use him to promote Patrón, and our guests' reactions to him confirmed our instincts. They were thrilled. It was a successful dry run for the Spago lunch, as Simon was to be our featured performer at the event.

The next day, I was both excited and petrified. Everything was on the line. But the room, in Spago's original Sunset Boulevard location, looked flawless. Wolfgang created a selection of hors d'oeuvres and an exquisite three-course lunch menu using Patrón as an ingredient in each item. Nothing like this had ever been done before. His *amuses bouches* and sorbets were almost as talked about as our giant leap of faith in Patrón itself. While the 100-plus guests mingled, sipped, and murmured in anticipation, Simon was on hand to perform tricks and wow them at their tables, charming everyone just as we expected he would.

While the judges huddled together on one side of the dining room, the party was raging on the other, which was packed with tastemakers and members of the press. Out of the corner of my eye I could see Martin pacing. He'd briefly lost his confidence and was sweating profusely. For a man so full of bravado, it was unusual to see him that nervous. But then, everything was at stake.

You wouldn't know it to look at John Paul, who was perfectly calm.

"JP, aren't you worried?" I asked him.

"Not at all, Ilana. We've got this; I just know it," he said.

Ernst & Young went upstairs to tally the scores and then came back down with a verdict. The suspense was unbearable. Although we knew no one could match us in taste, we'd put ourselves up against the most expensive and recognized brands at the time: Herradura, Sauza Commemorativo, and some of the Cuervo tequilas, among those I can recall. It was a small pool to choose from in those days. Of course Patrón was the most expensive of the competing brands and therefore the only one paying attention to packaging and presentation in addition to quality.

But we were still taking a tremendous risk, so to say I had butterflies would be an understatement. Finally, one of the auditors called everyone's attention, and announced:

"And the winner is. . . ."

Just at that moment, Simon the magician lit a cigarette, creating a poof of smoke from which a bottle of Patrón appeared. It was our big finale. (Of course, Simon had the other brands stashed nearby in case a different winner was announced.)

JP was right. We came out on top. The crowd roared in approval, and the press garnered over the next few days and weeks was phenomenal. The event put us on the map. Passing the blind test gave us the right to claim that we were the best-tasting tequila on the market.

At five o'clock, the last of our lunch guests poured out of Spago and into the limos we'd hired to get them safely home. From then on, Patrón was on the lips of every hipster in Hollywood.

A star was born.

A PERFECT SCIENCE

For all the beauty of the packaging and the hype of its high-profile fans, Patrón would be nothing without the unique taste. That's why one of the first things Martin did when he discovered the original factory was to make the Patrón recipe proprietary, consulting closely with Francisco to adjust the distillation process to make the taste even smoother. That move proved essential to Patrón's enduring success as the market leader. As the brand expanded into a number of products and we had to adapt a few of the processing methods to our growing business, no single step in production over the last two decades was ever compromised, and the one thing that never changed in the making of Patrón was the taste.

It begins with the agave. All tequila is made from the distillation and fermentation of agave. Contrary to popular misconception, agave is not a cactus but a succulent related to the lily family. Scientifically known as the *Agave tequilana* Weber Azul, after the German botanist who studied and classified the agave family of plants at the beginning of the last century, blue agave is a giant of a plant, growing up to 12 feet in diameter, with a life span of up to 15 years.

IDEAL CONDITIONS

As in the vineyards of Burgundy, not all agave fields are created equal. Just as with grapes, certain plots of land have superior growing conditions and soil. Francisco uses the French wine-growing term *terroir* to describe the differences. Loosely translated as "a sense of place," it refers to the special features of a location, including geography, geology, climate, and all those other factors that make up a local environment and combines with the genetics of the plant to create a unique product.

The volcanic subsoils and microclimates of Jalisco contribute to the nuance of flavor, which tends to be earthier in the lowlands, where the sugar content is lower, and fruitier from the agave grown in the highlands, which has a greater sugar content. Agave for Patrón is grown in the highlands, and Francisco travels to each farm, maintaining close ties with the owners and laborers in the fields he buys from so that no important information affecting the outcome of the agave crop will be missed. In fact, Patrón maintains long-term contracts with a number of top agave farmers in the area.

Agave requires a highly specialized type of farming, and not all farmers are as skilled in the tricky business of cultivating and harvesting agave. It takes the Blue Weber variety 6 to 10 years to mature before the sugar contents peak, making it ripe for harvest, and only the *jimador*—the agave farmer—knows when the succulent is ready. It is crucial, because harvesting at the wrong time, when the sugar levels are not perfect, can ruin a batch of tequila. Harvest too soon, and it can taste bitter; too late, and it tastes like an overripe fruit.

FATHER TO SON

When it's the right time, the *jimador* discards the flower, which helps condense the sap inside the heart of the plant. There's a whole science to this process, and only a handful of agave farmers truly understand the tradition, which is passed down from father to son. Agave farming families dedicate their lives to mastering this art, which has been practiced the same way for centuries. The *jimadores* even have their own implement, a *coca de jima*, a flat-bladed knife at the end of a long pole that's used to slice off the sharp, bitter leaves, or *pencas*, of the agave plant, leaving behind the sweet heart, or *pina*.

Then it's time to select the agaves. Only those with the right balance of sugar and acid are chosen. Francisco uses all of his senses and some technology to determine which are the best, individually testing each small lot of harvested *pinas* by cutting and removing a piece of the core to make sure the sugar content is exactly right.

Once the finest agave *pinas* are selected and trimmed, they are delivered to the distillery, where they are quartered and put in traditional masonry ovens and, as described in detail on the Patrón website, they are slowly steamed in small batches for 79 hours.[1] Some brands cook the *pinas* more quickly in huge industrial kilns called autoclaves, but Patrón still uses brick ovens for slow roasting. Also, unlike other tequilas, Patrón removes the bitter kernel inside the heart of the agave before it's processed, which contributes to the unique smoothness. Throughout the baking process, special stokers keep track of the oven's fire, keeping it steady to ensure a consistent temperature. The more gradually the *pinas* are cooked, the more concentrated the flavor is.

When they are removed from the kilns, the steamed *pinas* ooze with rich sweetness, much like the bleeding heart of the agave goddess Mayahuel of the Aztec legend. Once softened, these dark brown, honeyed chunks of cooked agave are shredded and then placed in a shallow traditional stone pit, where they are macerated with a large stone milling wheel that rotates on its own axis. The wheel turns inside a special *tahona*, a small circular space made of heavy cantera stone hewn from a nearby mountain. The resulting paste is diluted with water from a natural unique spring-fed deep well situated on the property, which also contributes to Patrón's refined taste. Since Francisco first developed the recipe for Patrón with Martin in 1989, he has been using a combination of tahona crushed and shredded agave produced by a mechanical shredder, creating subtle complexities detectable to the most discerning palates. [2]

The juice from the agave is then placed in wooden fermentation tanks for 72 hours. Fermentation is the conversion of sugars into alcohol, a delicate and complex process that one tequila factory tries to help along by piping classical music into the fermentation rooms.[3] It is said that the rhythm of the music promotes yeast growth, although it is more likely a gimmick for the amusement of modern-day tequila tourists. The fermented mixture, which is called *must*, is then distilled twice in traditional copper pot stills. The first distillation produces a sweet, low-alcohol brew. The second distillation is less sweet and has a much higher alcohol content. After distillation, each batch is finely filtered and balanced under Francisco's constant and exacting supervision.

AN EVOLVING ART

By continuing to use these proven ancient methods, Patrón not only is honoring tradition, it's retaining each step in the process to maintain the sublime flavor of the tequila Martin discovered and refined. From the time spent on each step to the temperature, mechanics, and materials that come into contact with the agave, it's not just one ingredient that's the key to its recipe; it's every stage in the way the tequila is made.

Of course, a few things have evolved over time. It's no trade secret that Patrón no longer uses mules to pull the *tahona*. The original Patrón factory was the only one in Mexico that had a mule-drawn stone mill, but as charmingly anachronistic as the use of these animals may be, their absence does not affect the final outcome. There have been some slight changes in the fermentation process that have introduced some extremely subtle differences, and some would argue improvements, to the original. The agave is also sourced from several different fields in Jalisco. As a result, there are nuanced differences in taste, though not quality, compared with the original, but they are discernible by only the most expert tequila aficionados.[4]

Martin and Francisco first noticed how the slightest change can affect a batch of tequila when a second factory was built by the same family near the original location to keep up with our ever-growing orders. The new facility combined state-of-the-art equipment with Francisco's old-school distilling methods, but it couldn't quite duplicate the taste of the first, with its donkey-driven stone and decades-old vats.

It's always a risk when you grow. You can do everything exactly right and follow a precise pattern, but when it comes to a sublime product such as Patrón, there is always an unquantifiable element that's hard to control. But neither Martin nor Francisco would accept defeat. To bridge the difference, they quickly came up with the idea of blending the Patrón from the new factory with the Patrón from the old factory. It finally passed their exacting taste test, and for years afterward they used this solution. These were minor adjustments that in no way altered the authenticity and superb quality of a brand that has become a testimony to what can be done when old school craftsmanship meets modern ingenuity.

How long the tequila ages results in the different categories. The most recognized types of tequila are Blanco (White) or Plata (Silver), unaged and bottled immediately; Reposado, aged over two months; and Anejo, aged a minimum of one year. Oak barrels are used for aging; this is what gives the Anejo tequila the amber color and smoky flavor. Today, Patrón has ultrapremium tequilas that are aged even longer and triple distilled, and the competition has been following suit.

FROM STILL TO SHELF

Once it has been distilled, filtered, and aged, the tequila is bottled on the premises. The ovens used to make Patrón bottles were designed specifically to produce them. A glass artisan employed by the factory measures the amount of glass used to make a bottle by hand, using the traditional skills of glassmaking passed on to an apprentice from a master. As with the *jimadores*, the art of producing these exquisite glass vessels is passed down through families. Each bottle is unique and individually handmade by an artisan schooled in the art of glass-blowing. In keeping with Patrón's environmentally conscious policies, the well-known bottles for Silver, Reposado, and Anejo are still fashioned from recycled glass.

As part of the process, each bottle is individually washed in tequila before it is filled. This creates the proper environment to receive Patrón, coating the glass and ensuring that no debris or impurities taint its contents. From the birth of our brand, each bottle was designed to be a piece of art, fit to hold the world's finest tequila. Workers individually number and sign each label, hand-tie ribbons, and wipe the bottle free of dust. The final product is cradled in paper and boxed before being sent around the world to be enjoyed by tequila enthusiasts. While the packaging does not affect the contents, the beauty of every detail does enhance the unique experience of drinking Patrón. It is the external manifestation of all the time, care, and precision that went into the crafting of its contents.

Patrón's journey can take more than a decade from a seedling in an agave field to an artfully packaged bottle of ultrapremium tequila. In addition to the time the agave requires to ripen, it can take another two to three years for the production and manufacturing of tequila. For the spirit to be classified as tequila, it must have at least 51 percent of its fermented sugars extracted from the Weber Azul. Anything less and it cannot be sold as tequila. Patrón uses 100 percent, and it was the first on the U.S. market to do so.

SILVER STANDARD

The proof of these monumental efforts to produce greatness comes down to that initial sip. Patrón was the first brand in which the Silver actually surpassed sales of the Gold because of both its smoothness, which does not exist in other Blanco tequilas, and the bold flavor of the agave fruit, with notes of citrus herbs and the slightest earthy quality. It has what the Japanese call *umami*, a delicious savory note almost like that of a mushroom. Patrón in its purest form, the Silver, surprises all who try it with a crisp clean finish that belies the subtle complexity of its flavors.

Personally, I love the Silver best, but everyone has his or her favorite. The Reposado layers onto the smoothness of the Silver a slightly smoky, almost peppery taste, and the Gold, or Anejo, has an almost buttery, smooth finish with a hint of oak.

Just as with any great wine, single malt, or cognac, the unique character that lies within each variation of Patrón depends on the methods of baking, fermenting, distilling, and aging, as well as the environment, temperature, type of soil, and equipment used to make the spirit. But I have left out one other determining element in the greatness of Patrón: its people.

THE ARISTOCRAT

I shall start with the individual who is arguably the brand's most essential ingredient. An impeccable gentleman and a glorious human being, Francisco Alcaraz is Patrón's man with the platinum palate. Never satisfied until the last bottle of a batch is filled, sealed, and packaged, he looks, tastes, and smells Patrón at every moment in the production process. His muscle memory for the many thousands of batches he produced throughout the years is extraordinary There is no pretension. He doesn't even drink from a special tequila glass because he fears that opening the bouquet in a fine crystal snifter would make the Patrón inside too delicious for objectivity.

"If something is wrong, I want to taste it!" he says.[5]

Watching Francisco is like observing a true artist in action. He studies the contents of his glass, staring down the center to determine its color and gently turning the tequila around to see how it clings to the sides. Just like a master sommelier, he swirls his glass before tasting to open it up, then sips, holding the liquid in his mouth for almost a minute to measure each note as it bursts on his tongue. But the difference between a sommelier in the wine industry and Francisco is that there is no one else quite like him among makers of tequila.

The connection Martin felt with this old school Spanish gem was instant. When Martin and JP joked about what tequila Mexican aristocrats drink, they never expected they'd encounter an actual aristocrat on that remote hillside in Jalisco. But Francisco stood out as a connoisseur with an acute appreciation for life's finest, just like Martin. In many ways, they were soul brothers. Although Martin's manner could be gruff and bombastic next to Francisco's quiet and gentle demeanor, they had the utmost respect for each other.

Francisco also lent a critical technical expertise to our business. He is a trained scientist and was at the forefront of the modernization and standardization of Mexico's tequila industry. In 1968, he was appointed the first tequila inspector by the Mexican Government Commerce and Industry Secretary (SECOFI). It was his job to monitor Mexico's distilleries closely to ensure that each met the minimum requirements for agave content and held to the increasingly strict requirements for production. In fact, Francisco raised the bar for everyone.

In 1982, he became an independent consultant and served as professor at CBTIS College, the *Centro de Bachillerato Tecnologico Industrial y de Servicios*, a national chain of high-level technical schools offering programs for degree holders to obtain professional-level credentials. In other words, he trained the next generation of industry inspectors. He was then brought in to design the Pernod Ricard Distillery in Mexico. Around 1989, he was lured to the original Patrón factory as a full-time consultant.

Over the years, Francisco has observed the growth of the tequila industry and the fervor of the U.S. consumer with quiet bemusement. The relatively recent phenomenon of mixology, in which bartenders go to elaborate lengths to assemble the perfect cocktail using the most exotic ingredients imaginable, seems redundant to Francisco when Patrón alone is already perfection.

"When we drink tequila in Mexico, it is still served in the same way as when I was a young man," he was quoted as saying in an interview with the *Houston Press*.[6] "We serve it straight, with lime and salt, or with *sangrita* [a spicy fruit/tomato juice chaser]."

In Mexico, tequila is what friends drink when they gather to celebrate or watch a soccer match. Just as the host in many cultures immediately offers guests a cup of tea when they enter a home, the tequila glasses come out for visitors in middle- and upper-class homes throughout Mexico. It is generally served with snacks such as nuts or slices of cheese. Fine tequila is almost never mixed, and when it is, the taste should not be masked with tart, overly sweetened mixers but enhanced by complementary ingredients. More than once, when we entertained our dear friend, Francisco would raise his eyebrows at some of Martin's more creative use of Patrón in food and cocktails. But after some good-natured teasing, he would be pleasantly surprised by Martin's latest concoctions.

Like Martin, Francisco often suffered from frail health. At one point, when Francisco was staying with us in Anguilla on business, he had to be rushed to the hospital. A few hours earlier, Martin had to be taken to another emergency room for heart arrhythmia. I was running between the two rooms, terrified that these two beloved men in my life were at death's door, and neither of them knew the other was ill. Francisco didn't want Martin to be upset and vice versa, so I wasn't allowed to say anything to either of them. Happily, Francisco is alive and well. Although he has some well-groomed successors to carry on his art whenever he leaves, I can't imagine that he'll ever choose retirement. He loves Patrón too much.

THE MARKETING MASTER

Not every human ingredient in Patrón plays a physical role in production. Our Patrón family added a certain intangible spirit to the brand that made it special above and beyond the packaging and its contents. John Paul was and is just as much a part of its DNA.

Martin could not have found a more perfect partner for building a brand, because JP had been there once before. Through John Paul Mitchell Systems, he knew what it took to build a consumer brand that no one else believed in. Like Martin, he came from a broken home and built up his fortune from nothing. His family had no money. There were no connections to help him on his way.

JP was an impoverished street kid who had to work hard his entire life. Born to immigrant parents from Italy and Greece, he was raised in different parts of Los Angeles, including areas rife with crime and violent street gangs. As a child, he and his brother would get up at three in the morning to fold and deliver newspapers to help support their family. It reached the point where, for one and a half years, his single mother had difficulty supporting the children, so they were sent into foster care during the week, but were home on weekends.

After a brief stint in the U.S. Navy, JP reentered civilian life a divorced single father struggling to survive. He did whatever odd jobs he could find to support himself and his son, selling everything from encyclopedias, to photocopy machines, to life insurance. A few times he found himself homeless and sleeping in his car. But he doesn't regret a thing about those lean years. Going door to door helped him build his vast repertoire as a marketer and salesman and taught him the power of persistence. There is nothing like having countless doors slammed in your face to make or break your confidence, and by the end, JP could talk just about anyone into giving him a chance. The man simply oozes charm and charisma. He has a way of making anyone he is speaking with feel like the most important person in the room.

Before long, JP had hustled his way into *TIME* magazine's marketing department, where he quickly worked his way up from a junior position to head of circulation for Los Angeles. From there, he moved to Redken Laboratories, the top professional hair care brand at the time, with a starting salary of $600 a month. After 18 months he was put in charge of two sales divisions, including schools and salons, and succeeded in multiplying revenues. Along the way, he formed a friendship with the top hair stylist Paul Mitchell. In 1980, with a loan of $700, they launched John Paul Mitchell Systems.

Together, the two men created a whole new market that catered to hairstylists. In keeping with JP's environmentalist passion, they were the first such products not to be tested on animals. To overcome skepticism in the marketplace, JP started knocking on doors again, this time at salons, offering free demonstrations and offering to take back all unsold products at no cost to the salons. He guaranteed sales, something that had never been done in the industry. It was a struggle, and for the first few months JP and his partner could barely cover their bills as JP went all over the country, sleeping in his car yet again. But in a few short years they built JPMS into a business worth hundreds of millions.

In the early years, JP was best known for his hair care business. Often, when we were traveling together, even in obscure places such as Anguilla and Cuba, people would point at him and say, "Paul Mitchell, Paul Mitchell!" thinking that was his name. But he has since gone on to build or invest in numerous other successful and wide-ranging businesses in addition to being an internationally recognized philanthropist and environmental activist. It's his ability to find opportunity where no one else is looking and his persistence and passionate commitment to everything he undertakes that make him an extraordinary businessman and human being. As JP likes to say, "The difference between successful people and unsuccessful people is that successful people do a lot of the things that unsuccessful people don't want to do."[7]

In many ways, Martin and JP were cut from the same cloth. As different as their personalities were—Martin was all rough edges next to JP's smooth persona—JP recognized a little of his old hard-scrabble self in Martin when they first came into each other's lives in 1989. They'd been introduced by a mutual friend, Jack Mahoney, who brought Martin to JP's house in Beverly Hills for a dinner party. JP was in the process of finalizing plans to build his Malibu estate at the time. Martin gave JP his business proposal seeking an investor for APM, his import-export business. As part of the deal, JP could get any of the APM sourced materials he needed for building the Malibu house at cost plus 10 percent. The savings alone would cover his investment, so it wasn't a huge risk. They became equal partners, and APM was born.

THE VISIONARY

Martin was a born entrepreneur. He was constantly coming up with ideas, most of which came to fruition despite the doubts of onlookers. He had little in the way of formal education and training, yet it seemed he could do just about anything he set his mind to. He was self-taught, a natural prodigy.

The oldest of three children, he came from a dreary small town in central California. Money was scarce. His father had abandoned the family when Martin was in his early teens, and his mother chose to cling to her misery ever afterward. Martin couldn't wait to leave and struck out on his own at age 17. By 22, he'd made his first million.

He spent the rest of his adult life living large and dreaming big, racing yachts and avidly collecting everything from racehorses to high-performance cars, art, and fine wines. He had discerning taste in all things, and he surrounded himself with beauty. Though a child of the 1960s who never missed a chance to indulge the many whims of his free and fun-loving spirit, Martin was above all a businessman determined to succeed.

He had a special knack for recognizing a need and turning it into an opportunity in which everyone came out ahead. It didn't matter what arena he was operating in. Even as a young man in the eastern Caribbean's Peace Corps, he soon learned that the villagers consumed a staggering amount of chicken, all of which was being imported. Before long, he had assembled the locals, taught them how to raise their own chickens, organized co-ops, assisted emerging ancillary enterprises, and ultimately empowered them to become self-sufficient. The result was multiple microbusinesses that served to elevate living standards in an impoverished region. Whether he was operating a winery in Napa or building his own house from the foundation in Carmel, Martin was never afraid to take risks, and fear was never a factor. He just knew how to get things done. It was all a challenge, and the exciting part was finding a creative solution. In Martin's world, the question was never if, but how.

By the time I met Martin, just a few months before his discovery of Patrón, he'd made—and lost—$8 million. He'd created a small empire in building, buying, and selling homes, hotels, restaurants, and a winery, but it all came crashing down when he leveraged his properties and overextended himself. He'd been humbled and became aware that there was more to life than the trappings of wealth. The timing was right for both of us. We were meant to meet when we did.

THE HELPMATE

I was born and raised in a tiny town outside of Johannesburg, South Africa, where I'd lived a sheltered life, excelling in school and dance competitions while being doted on by my father and my mother, a survivor of Auschwitz. They died three months apart from each other: my mother from a brain aneurysm and then my father from a heart attack. Looking back, I am sure he'd lost his will to live. I was 18.

Numb with grief, I took over and ran my mother's ladies clothing boutique, with the help of Len, my brother-in-law, and my older sister, Sharon. My twenties were a blur: I got married, then divorced, closed the store, took a position working for Len in his new clothing manufacturing business, then became the personal assistant and executive secretary to the president of a record label in Johannesburg. I had adjusted to life without parents, keeping myself too busy to think. Then Sharon and Len decided to immigrate to America with their two small sons. I was devastated, although I understood why they wanted to leave. There didn't seem to be much of a future in South Africa under apartheid. But they were all the family I had. We were incredibly close, and I loved them dearly.

Feeling abandoned, I took off and traveled the world for two years. I lived in London most of the time, venturing all over Europe from there. I also visited my sister and family in Los Angeles for a few months. After everything I'd experienced, I was a changed individual by the time I returned to South Africa. It was not possible for me to continue living there.

My inner circle from the music industry was multiracial—black, Indian, and white—and we defied government segregation rules by dining and socializing together, albeit behind closed doors. I wasn't political in any way, but the institutionalized racism was deeply troubling to me and Jo'burg began to feel suffocatingly small. It was time to leave and join my family in California.

I arrived in the United States with nothing but $200 in cash and a small suitcase. After a dramatic entry in which I was pulled out of the immigration queue at JFK airport for no apparent reason and nearly sent back to South Africa, I hit the ground running. To get my green card and stay in America, I immediately landed a job in Los Angeles with Norman Winter, the famed publicist who handled the likes of CBS, Sony, 3M, Michael Jackson, and Elton John. In exchange for a green card and a meager $120 a week, I repaid him by working long hours and doing whatever was needed to keep his office running. In return, Norman's agency introduced me to the decadent world of drugs, parties, and celebrity. I was shy and somewhat sheltered in my upbringing, even growing up without a television. Generally unimpressed by fame, I found myself thrust into the epicenter of Hollywood life at the height of the disco era, when cocaine and Quaaludes were distributed around the office like Post-it notes.

But I was still marking time in an office, and I hated it. When Len offered me a position as sales rep to launch his commercial office supply operation, paid by commission, I leaped at the chance for independence. Loving my newfound freedom, I pounded the pavement, going door to door, canvassing every office, law firm, and movie studio that would let me past its gate or reception desk. I quickly realized that in America everything really *is* bigger, especially the opportunities. The dollar amounts were like phone numbers. Within months, I'd built up the business, networking and building relationships with Fox Studios and other major clients around town.

It wasn't long before the office supply business was running itself. With so much free time on my hands and a natural facility for numbers, I needed another challenge. When a girlfriend suggested that I join her financial consulting company, I wasted no time getting my license and building up a financial and retirement advisory business for teachers. Within a few years, I had over 700 clients and was making more than a quarter of a million a year. By the time I hit my mid-thirties I was comfortable and reasonably content with my lot in life.

But there was always something missing. My romantic relationships never seemed to last more than three years, and each one that failed sent my self-esteem into a deeper spiral. The last one to crash and burn sent me on a soul-searching mission. It suddenly occurred to me that my emotions had been so suppressed after my parents died that I no longer knew how I felt. I was just catapulting from one relationship to the next without giving myself the chance to grieve. So I put my love life on hiatus and after ten years returned to South Africa, where I visited my parents' graves and cried like never before.

CHEMICAL ROMANCE

Everything up to that point was preparing me for Martin. After going a year without a man in my life, friends were starting to worry. One in particular, Pam Orenstein, was determined to help me end my reclusive phase and invited me to a small wine-tasting gathering at her home. She had a surprise in store for me: a man whose extravagant lifestyle she'd often spoken of would also be there. Although I'd never met him, I'd already decided I didn't like him. Extravagance is nice only when you're indulging in it yourself.

But my preconceptions were a poor defense. I didn't stand a chance. When Martin walked into that room, it was impossible not to notice him. He was tall, barrel-chested, and not well dressed, but with his shaggy mane of dark hair and flashing brown eyes he had an imposing presence that was irresistible. He looked like a better looking Irish version of Gene Simmons, but with beautiful hair, a type I find appealing. Martin locked his eyes with mine and came toward me like a heat-seeking missile. The attraction was immediate, but it wasn't physical as much as intellectual. From the first moment we were engaged in a verbal sparring match that was electric. To call it flirting would be an understatement. We went home together, and thus began a 13-year love affair like none I'd known before or since.

Martin opened up a side of me I didn't know existed: he single-handedly put me in touch with my creativity. He encouraged me and gave me the confidence to take it as far as it would go. But it was more than that. Somehow, we had made the union of a lifetime. It was truly a case of the sum being greater than the parts. I softened Martin's edges, and in return he became my most ardent fan, helping me rebuild my self-esteem and making me feel like anything was possible. Whether in loving and loving well or in nurturing a business like no other, we were so much better together than apart.

YIN AND YANG

Individually, we were far from perfect human beings, but we made each other better in so many ways. Even our worst qualities blended, complemented, and made us that much closer and stronger as a union. Recently, I drew up a list of our different qualities or ingredients, to better understand what it was about our contrasting personalities that meshed so well.

For me I wrote "a desire to please, shy, intelligent, credible, respected in business, organized, skilled marketer, competent, trusted, law-abiding, honest, helpful and loving." For Martin I listed "interesting, compelling, brash, brazen, self-absorbed, tough on the outside, bombastic, loving, caring, considerate, supportive, encouraging, wildly imaginative, a brilliant entrepreneur and designer." For us together I came up with "collaborative, complementary, infectious, indulgent, fun, socially outrageous, completely and utterly intertwined, each indistinguishable from the other, deeply in love, and sexually free." A mass contradiction in terms, to say the least.

In a way, Patrón symbolized all that was best in our relationship. We each possessed a unique mixture of characteristics and ingredients that, put together, made magic. Years later, our friend Caroline Law summed up our special alchemy succinctly as "a chemical romance cocktail." That's exactly what we were together: an intoxicating, potentially explosive combination of elements that probably should not have gone together and yet somehow did, beautifully.

"Ilana, I always knew Martin was going to go far, but you made it work," she told me. "You warmed him up and made him believable."

As a couple, we took a huge bite out of life. Without going into too much detail, we both liked to indulge and often pushed the envelope of convention. While we were spiritually faithful to each other and completely trusting, that did not rule out threesomes together. I am sexually free and enjoy women, but only in the context of a loving relationship with a man, and Martin was more than happy to indulge me. It led to some wildly romantic adventures.

I adored Martin despite and perhaps because of his many flaws and contradictions. He was like the Hindu god Shiva: yin and yang all rolled into one, a vibrant life force that creates as much as it destroys. In business he was aggressive, but in love he was soft and gentle, almost feminine. The man was a living, breathing paradox, as sensitive and spiritual as he was blindingly ambitious. He was a doer who played hard and a romantic partner with the most delicate sensibility of anyone I had ever met.

There was a profound tenderness in the way he treated me. No one outside our circle of close friends would ever believe it, but this was a man who left love notes and roses on my pillow for no reason at all. Many times, we would be driving past a field somewhere, and he would suddenly pull over, stop, leap out of the car, and pick me some wildflowers that happened to have caught his eye. I still have books full of pressed flowers he gave to me over the years.

We found any excuse to celebrate our lives together, but our biggest occasion was Valentine's Day. Early on in the relationship, before Patrón came our way and the money I earned was just enough,

I racked my brain to try to come up with something to mark the holiday that seemed designated just for us. I looked into hiring a plane to sky write the message "I love you, Martin," but it was prohibitively expensive. I researched romantic Caribbean getaways, but they were also beyond my budget. Finally, I decided to book a suite at a wonderful boutique hotel in Beverly Hills for the night. I called Martin at work to give him instructions for the evening. "Don't ask any questions; just show up at this address at six o'clock, when you've finished work," I told him.

At the end of my workday, I rushed home, packed my sexiest lingerie, and headed to the hotel to embellish the suite and set the mood. But Martin had already beaten me to it. When I walked into the room, there he was. Seductive music caressed the room, rose petals covered the bed, champagne had already been poured with strawberries resting on our glasses' rims, and the Jacuzzi was foaming over with mountains of bubbles. But the crowning surprise was Linda Blom, our friend and masseuse, who was ready with a massage table and delicious concoctions of oils and fragrances.

There was something palpable about the chemistry we shared. When we were enjoying a meal at a restaurant, a random couple came up to us and said, "So sorry for interrupting, but we just wanted to say we've been mesmerized by the connection between you. It's so apparent that you two are amazing together." It happened more than once.

Our generosity and passion for each other were inclusive. Friends and acquaintances on our path were swept up in our joy for life and welcomed our grand gestures. Martin was generous and enjoyed being able to indulge his creativity, and doing something special for friends was fun. The amount of effort and energy and attention to detail was because he loved the whole package. One time he provided cases of Patrón for a friend's huge wedding reception that had to be shipped across the country. Martin included hundreds of shot glasses, meticulously planning and executing a fabulous presentation. When the guests entered the reception hall, they were greeted with a shot of Patrón in their very own frosted glass that they continued to refill throughout the night. It was the one thing that everyone remarked on and remembered about that happy day.

We shared an energy and enthusiasm and were enamored with each other from the very beginning, before Patrón was even a thought, and it ignited and fueled an extraordinary romance that never died. In fact, it intensified the more time we spent together. There was never that dwindling passion couples have when they've been in a relationship for a few years. Somehow, we just fed off each other. It was effortless.

For 12 of our 13 years, Martin and I shared every inch of our beings together. We knew how to love and be loved, and we thrived on both, truly living for each other's pleasure. Seduction was present in everything we did, and our everyday life was as voluptuous and sensuous as could be. Throughout our relationship, we lived to delight each other with moments of magic, spontaneity, and mind-blowing gestures that thrilled. We made even the simplest pastimes seem special and never lost that sense of wonder for new things. Patrón became the benefactor of our exhilaratingly rare and racy relationship, because our passion and lust for life carried over into everything we did. Our lives were reflected in Patrón just as much as Patrón was reflected in our lives, so it's no surprise that it is such a sexy brand.

It's not just the ingredients that make something work, it's also timing. Martin was at a point in his life where he was ready for a helpmate, just as I was eager to embrace someone else's dream and make it happen. It was true for all of us. Whether you are lovers, friends, or simply business partners with a profound respect for each other's strengths, a true partnership can make the difference between something that's just good and an enterprise that is a phenomenal success. The essential elements of our brand—Francisco, Martin, JP, me, and of course the many hands that touched our product along the way—came together at a time when Patrón was simply meant to be. We all made up the perfect blend at the perfect moment.

There was one other key ingredient that made it magic: love.

PART II

BRAND BUILDING

CHAPTER 4

Hollywood Star

JOHN PAUL and Eloise DeJoria were relaxing in their new Malibu home one Saturday evening when out of the blue they got a call from one of their dear friends.

"What are you and Eloise doing tomorrow?" he asked.

"Nothing, Clint. Why?"

"Come to my movie premiere. I've got two tickets waiting for you. And a surprise."

JP thanked him profusely and showed up at the premiere, but Clint Eastwood wasn't there. JP and Eloise took their seats, still with no idea what the surprise might be unless it was the great seats, free popcorn, and soda. The film was *In the Line of Fire*, about a secret service agent, and the only thing this character drank was Patrón. In the movie's most intricate scene, when Clint's character is negotiating with a terrorist over the phone, Patrón gets a close-up that lasts about a minute.

A few months earlier, John Paul had sent Clint a case of Patrón. As Clint was such a big fan of our product, JP assumed it was for his private consumption. Lifestyle brands happily comp celebrities on the merest chance of a mention in interviews or on the red carpet.

But Clint was never one to abuse a friend's generosity. He is an old school gentleman, and he intended something much bigger for JP to show his appreciation: a close-up in a feature film. Most brands have to pay a fortune for product placement like that, but this was a gift.

A few years later, Clint did an interview with *Playboy* magazine, and when they asked him about his drink of choice, he replied: "Fine red wines and Patrón Tequila."

You couldn't buy better advertising than that.

THE A-LIST

We didn't have to. In the early 1990s, product placement for liquor companies was not entirely new, but it was rare, and brands had to pay six figures for a glimpse of their bottles on large and small screens. It was the other way around for Patrón. Because of its cachet as the only ultrapremium brand of tequila and the calculated risk we took with its high price point, Hollywood rolled out the red carpet for us. Of their own volition, stars who loved the brand asked Martin's permission to use Patrón in their movie scenes, even referring to it by name, and we didn't pay a dime.

Nor did we chase celebrity endorsements for Patrón. From the beginning, it was as if Patrón were the star and Hollywood's biggest names were its adoring fans. Being based in Southern California, it was only natural that the movie and entertainment industry would become an integral part of our diverse consumer landscape. It made perfect sense that the rest of the market would embrace Patrón as emblematic of the finer things in life the moment they saw America's equivalent of royalty sipping and enjoying our brand. Everyone wants to follow suit, because celebs surely know what's best. But to enter this rarefied circle, one must never try too hard. Patrón had to become the liquor of choice organically, through gradual recognition by the Hollywood cognoscenti. The bottle and its uniquely pure and crisp contents were their own glittering passport to fame.

We worked hard to build this profile. Getting into the VIP circles of Los Angeles was a calculated move, because the law of the land at that time prevented liquor companies from advertising on television. That made it necessary to come up with creative ways of raising visibility and getting the brand caught on film. We had to tap every connection available to us, slipping Patrón into every major Hollywood event and venue, from the Governors Ball at the Academy Awards to parties at the Grammys and Golden Globes. Within just two years of Martin's first discovery of the tequila that would become Patrón on a remote hillside in Jalisco, it had become the libation of choice at Playboy Mansion parties, film festivals, and award shows, getting top billing in movies and on television. Even rock icons like Jerry Garcia and Bruce Springsteen had it written into their contracts that Patrón be provided for them backstage while they were on tour.

The process began with John Paul, who brought a bottle of Patrón to every Hollywood event, party, and dinner that he and Eloise were invited to, which were many. One by one, he'd offer tastings in glasses of chilled crystal, each time garnering the same reaction: "Wow." This up-close and personal approach helped us enter the celebrity consciousness in a subtle way. But our star truly began to rise after that fabled lunch at Spago. The entire town was buzzing about our bravado and the now indisputable fact that Patrón was the best of the best.

Know who the true tastemakers are and use them wisely. Think about how anyone in your orbit, whether they are friends, members of the media, or product reviewers, can be best leveraged to promote your product. In the consumables business, word of mouth from fashionable and hip brand ambassadors speaks volumes to the mass market. But never, ever try too hard. You want your market to chase your brand, not the other way around.

HARD TO GET

In the beginning, two things helped create the sense that our product was highly covetable: scarcity and price. At $47 a bottle in the early days, Patrón was priced along the lines of fine Champagne, adding to the perception that it was a luxury to be sipped and savored. We still didn't have wide distribution and persistent production glitches meant that we could hardly keep up with the growing demand, so it was hard to find Patrón on the shelves. As a result, our distinctive bottle, festooned with its neon green or mango ribbon (for the Anejo) and silver- or gold-embossed labels, became a kind of all-access pass. After all, it's human nature to desire something rare and beautiful whether you are an A-lister or not.

Everything converged for the benefit of Patrón's exposure. JP garnered visibility and access for Patrón through his main business at the time, John Paul Mitchell Systems. Without having to pay a penny, we were able to piggyback on JPMS's many sponsored charity events, from televised celebrity golf tournaments to major national and international hair care conventions. This was highly unusual for a liquor brand at that time. Event sponsorship usually cost tens of thousands of dollars for the mere privilege of supplying free drinks, and it was one of only a few promotional options open for alcoholic beverage companies, given all the legal restrictions at the time.

FREE RIDE

On one occasion early on we were invited by JPMS to set up cocktail bars and preside over a massive gathering of John Paul Mitchell stylists and company staff. That move instantly gave us hundreds of enthusiastic brand ambassadors around the country. It was pure marketing genius. Next to bartenders, who better to influence a large captive audience of customers than hairdressers?

As a standard form of product promotion, JP would organize celebrity sporting invitationals all over the country, including volleyball tournaments, golf matches, skiing, broom hockey, and Jet Ski races. It was yet another thing the celebrities didn't have to pay for. JPMS would underwrite their holidays, which included celebrity chef-prepared dinners, parties, and entertainment for a week of fun, culminating in an auction to raise money for one of JP's many causes. Patrón would be included in certain of these celebrity sporting invitationals. Most of those events were taped and sold to cable TV, providing enormous coverage for our collective brands. Friends of John Paul's who were regulars at these occasions included Kevin Costner, Mick Fleetwood, Pierce Brosnan, Sean Penn, Dennis Hopper, and Peter Fonda, who all loved to party, along with countless others I can't recall. Peter and John Paul were and still are biker buddies. JP is a Harley-Davidson fan and often takes his Patrón-branded and -fueled bike out on the road with his *Easy Rider* friend.

One of our celebrity junkets was in Puerto Rico for the Christopher Reeve Foundation. That man worked diligently to raise money for his charity and maintained a positive spirit in the face of unimaginable physical challenges. We rarely saw Chris except at dinner and for various fund-raising activities. He spent much of his time in his hotel room undergoing intense physical therapy. He couldn't go anywhere without an army of nurses, occupational therapists, and assistants just to function in ways the rest of us take for granted. Obviously, he wasn't drinking Patrón, but his faithful old friend Robin Williams, who accompanied him on this trip, loved the stuff.

They were an odd couple. Robin was off the wall—exactly how you see him on television—entertaining for a minute, but the constant verbal onslaught could get tedious, so one tended to avoid him. You couldn't have a conversation without Robin taking some random thing you said and running with it. Yet he was genuinely devoted to Christopher and lived to make him laugh. They'd been the best of mates since long before Chris's horse riding accident, and you could feel the love between them. Robin's tenderness toward his friend was deeply touching.

In many ways, I was still the girl from South Africa who grew up without a television. Often, I found myself speaking with celebrities without having a clue who they were until it was pointed out to me afterward. But I enjoyed being in those exclusive environments. It felt like we'd arrived. We rubbed shoulders with the famous and infamous and clicked with a few people who became regulars at our dinner parties and celebrations.

Martin became especially close with James Coburn, who shared his passion for Eastern mysticism. Even I had my favorites. Having worked in the music industry both in South Africa and when I was at Norman Winter, I was a rock 'n' roll girl, and one of my dearest friends during our heyday was the late Clarence Clemons of Bruce Springsteen's E Street Band. We actually met waiting to use the restroom at a restaurant in Little Italy, New York. Martin and I were there with our friend John Capra, who knew the owner, and we were having a blast. Clarence walked right up to me and asked, "Are you the lady with Patrón? That's my favorite drink." I couldn't believe it was him. "Aren't you Clarence Clemons?" I squealed. He joined us at our table, we shut the place down, and Clarence, Martin, and I became fast friends. He even flew in to celebrate my forty-fifth birthday and serenaded me with his saxophone at my party.

But for these rare and special friendships, we didn't dive into the Hollywood scene for its own sake. Playing volleyball or skiing with such fascinating characters was always great fun, but we were much more interested in the net result of these junkets and parties: exposure. Our Patrón signage was seen by millions of viewers when these celebrity-sprinkled sporting events were shown on cable and network channels. It was invaluable for imprinting our brand on people's consciousness.

PINK DOLLARS

Martin and Dick Weaver often clashed over marketing tactics, and one of the most memorable occurred over Dick's insistence that Patrón be introduced to the gay community. Martin wanted nothing to do with it. It wasn't homophobia so much as reluctance to focus on any particular demographic, and his plate was already full with other promotion priorities. Martin kept putting off Dick's advances, saying that the market was a small one compared with the big picture and that the gay consumer would come to Patrón as a matter of course. He went so far as to instruct Dick not to actively promote Patrón to the bustling bar scene in West Hollywood.

On a marketing level Dick knew Martin might be right, but on a PR level he disagreed. He felt that for a product as hot as Patrón, the tone had to be set within the trendsetting gay scene before it was set for us. He feared that ignoring the gay community could be taken as a snub and might have disastrous consequences. He ignored Martin and started bringing bottles of Patrón to the bartenders and hosts of the most upscale venues and high-end gay events around town. When Martin found out, he was exasperated, but the strategy was producing results, so he allowed it to continue as long as Dick promised not to target the gay press or garner attention in a specific gay event, as our whole strategy was to avoid overtly targeting any specific group. Dick agreed. It was a rare moment of compromise between the two. Recently, JP told me that he has also always subscribed to the principle of marketing to all groups of people and not leave anyone out. He and Martin were unified on that front.

As for getting Patrón onto the big and small screens, we were lucky. In addition to John Paul's personal friendships in Hollywood, Dick put Patrón on the radar of Luis Barajas, the colorful founder and editor of *Detour* magazine, which has morphed into *Flaunt*, two of the hottest lifestyle glossies in Los Angeles. Luis was both a personal friend and a client of Dick's agency. Seeing the potential, Luis had become a huge fan of Patrón. Luis and Dick were part of the hip West Hollywood underground who had entrée everywhere, and it just so happened that Luis was always throwing the hottest parties LA had ever seen for his advertisers, among them the major studios. Ever the gregarious one, Dick would roam the red carpet, making sure a bottle of Patrón was put into the hand of a willing celebrity every time the *Entertainment Tonight* cameras were rolling.

Ed Blinn, who became our head of sales, once said in an interview, "If you go to six premieres and at every one they're serving Patrón, by the third you are drinking Patrón."[1] But it didn't even take that long to catch the attention of a number of actors and directors.

Luis was a particularly invaluable ally in those early days. Usually, studios would just hire someone to handle all the catering for their events, but Luis was especially hands-on about the way those legendary parties were managed, because they reflected on the reputation of his magazine. It was a given that he would choose to feature his favorite drink at every major red carpet event, including the Oscar night Governors Ball and the *Vanity Fair* party two years running. We were always prominently featured and included in the lavish swag baskets·for those and many other high-end show business events.

In return for supplying Patrón, we were given prime placement in heavily discounted full-page ads in Luis's magazine, which wielded considerable influence with the "right" people. Not everyone got into *Detour*. Luis was notorious for turning down countless brands and ungodly sums of money for placement because of his unflinching eye. Ours was an exchange of goods and services unheard of at the time, and *Detour*'s were the only consumer ads we ran.

Most sponsors at these Hollywood events not only provided everything for free, they had to pay a placement fee just to be there, but we were the exception, which only added to the aura. Through this simple barter system, our advertising budget for the first four years of Patrón's existence was minuscule. We had the mystique of being part of the inner circle, providing Patrón to private events through connections like the producers of shows such as *Entertainment Tonight, E!,* and *Extra* and the PR representative of the Hearst family, who made sure Patrón was available during parties at Hearst Castle and the family's other estates.

We networked at the highest levels, using every relationship we had and cultivating new ones. Because we had access to exclusive events and appeared in places where everyone wanted to be, the image of Patrón would appear in magazines or in the backdrops of television interviews—just enough to intrigue anyone who caught a glimpse of our bottle. Not that we had a detailed plan of attack. We simply hit the ground running, responding to every situation and opportunity in a way that seemed best for the brand.

SWAG

We dedicated many bottles to product sampling. When Dick was first hired to do our publicity, Martin provided him with multiple cases to sample with his Hollywood hipster friends. The crates that Patrón is shipped in were large and bulky to accommodate our generously proportioned bottles and packaging, which Dick put to good use by building a desk, a coffee table, and a sofa out of the boxes. A lot of product was used as samples, but it paid off. Tasting is believing, and before long we'd converted a legion of brand ambassadors.

Among those converts was Lara Flynn Boyle, one of the hot young actresses of the day, who was just coming off her success as a star of the hit David Lynch series *Twin Peaks*. She fell in love with Patrón after the Spago event. She was also a friend of Dick's who just happened to be dating his flat mate, Jeffrey Dean Morgan, at the time, so they'd shared many outrageous evenings together in his West Hollywood loft, getting high on Patrón. During one of their Patrón-fueled nights in a hotel room at the Chateau Marmont, Lara asked Dick if she could use Patrón in her next feature film, *Threesome*. The director, Andrew Fleming, was apparently also a fan of ours and wanted to feature the bottle in a sex scene between Lara and her costars Josh Charles and Stephen Baldwin involving body shots of Patrón. Dick was ecstatic. Martin was appalled.

"Body shots?! Dick, what are you on? That's not the message we are trying to send. Hell, no!"

"Martin, this is the opportunity of a lifetime. I don't care if they drink it out of a funnel as long as we get the bottle up on the screen."

The two got into a screaming match, as they often did when they disagreed. It was a love-hate relationship between the love of my life and one of my oldest friends, with a little more of the latter than the former. Both men were creative and passionate, and they clashed all the time. But Martin knew better than anyone where we were going with Patrón, and he was eager to rein Dick in. We had no objection to the movie's premise of three attractive college coeds engaging in a three-way. But the purpose of licking salt off someone's naked body part, shooting tequila, and then sucking a lime was to get drunk and hide the noxious taste of those cheap tequilas of the past. The scene would have associated Patrón with everything we were trying to get away from in people's perceptions of drinking tequila. Dick's argument was that the film was an art house project that would be seen by trendy upscale filmgoers, thereby widening the market. "Those tastemakers are tomorrow's luxury brand buyers," he insisted. But Martin was absolutely correct in his decision to tread a cautious line. It was vital to portray Patrón as a product of refinement, not drunken debauchery.

Dick ignored Martin's objections once again, and Patrón appeared in the movie, which was widely panned by critics. But surprisingly, *Threesome* had a decent showing at the box office and was seen by millions of young movie fans, so our baby's first sex scene in a feature film did indeed bring it to the attention of a broad national audience, however dubious the story line. It was the biggest splash Patrón had made thus far, and of course ours was the featured drink at all the movie premiere parties; thus, that single sex scene resulted in a generous amount of mileage for our brand. Soon requests were coming in from many other studios to use Patrón.

MORE CLOSE-UPS

One of movies vying for our bottle was Demi Moore's *Striptease*. The response was a firm "no, thank you" from Martin. Even Dick accepted that it would be wrong for us. We could afford to be selective and say no because we had the likes of David Bowie knocking at our door. The Bowie movie was called *The Linguini Incident*, a 1991 release also starring Marlee Matlin, Rosanna Arquette, and the stunning and delightful supermodel Iman, who became a friend of ours. In the film, Rosanna played an escape artist who plots with David Bowie's character to pull off a restaurant heist. Conveniently, he played a bartender, giving Patrón plenty of screen time in its supporting role. Again, an awful movie, but it helped to further launch us into the celebrity stratosphere.

Tom Cruise was another fan who requested Patrón as his co-star. The subject came up when we met him at a concert. He was just about to go into production for *Vanilla Sky*, a psychological thriller with a cast of impossibly beautiful actors, including Penelope Cruz and Cameron Diaz. Patrón is Tom's drink of choice in a notable bar scene in which he orders it multiple times, along with a beer chaser. Again, not our first choice for how the consumption of Patrón should be portrayed, but it was Tom Cruise, indisputably one of the finest actors in Hollywood.

During the filming he was staying at the Hotel Bel Air, where we sent him an assortment of Patrón-branded swag: some crystal glassware, cocktail shakers, a silver flask, a flip-top silver lighter emblazoned with our Patrón bee. They were what we called lifestyle accessories: objects collected as part of our research and development. We assumed it was the kind of gift celebrities receive all the time, but you wouldn't have thought so by Tom's reaction. He called to thank us with incredible warmth and sincerity, specifically noting the high quality of the items we sent. Stars of that caliber would never usually bother to make such a call. They'd have an assistant get in touch, if at all. But Tom was more gracious than most.

COLLECTOR'S ITEM

Celluloid was a big boost to our brand recognition, but there were other, less direct entries into Hollywood culture that we never intended. Suddenly, our empty bottles were appearing on the dinner tables and elsewhere in the finest homes in Beverly Hills. People were collecting the empties and using them for everything from flower vases and salad dressing shakers to bath salt dispensers. Our individually numbered, hand-signed vessels had become a hip at-home accessory, the more so whenever we had those periodic problems with production and distribution. In fact, people began bidding wars to access the empties, which sometimes cost more than a full bottle of Patrón, particularly for the lower numbers. In fact, I still see numerous ads for the sale of these empties on eBay and Craigslist, so the collectors' fever continues.

As a marketing ploy, it horrified Martin, as he feared it would detract from the bottle's contents.

"We're selling tequila, not objects d'art," he snapped at Dick.

But it certainly did not hurt our image to accept and exploit the idea that our painstakingly crafted packaging was becoming so eminently collectable. The bottle alone, distinctive and recognizable even without the Patrón label, was having an impact and building awareness at the highest levels. Thank God Martin had registered the design of the bottle from the moment he'd conceived it, because in its own side-door fashion it was fueling Patrón's growing status as an iconic brand. It wasn't enough that people were eager to taste our product. They never discarded the empty bottles.

Eventually Martin gave in. Too many Patrón fans were expressing their devotion to the brand in this unexpected way. He even began to encourage the collectors' frenzy. Every time we went into a bar or restaurant, he told the bartender or waiter that whoever bought the last drop out of a bottle of Patrón could keep the bottle. He had all our friends spread the word across the country, and it soon became quite a fad at certain hip, high-end restaurants.

Celebrities were among the most passionate collectors of Patrón bottles. Actress Anjelica Huston's late husband, Robert Graham, who was a brilliant sculptor, asked for the empties so that he could create a wall out of them. It was a charming request, so how could we not oblige? Bruce Springsteen was so distraught when his low-numbered empties were destroyed during the Northridge earthquake that Martin produced duplicates to replace his lost treasures. We had to accept the fact that our fans saw Patrón as much more than just an ultrapremium spirit. To them, it was also art.

GOING GLOBAL

What they lacked in numbers initially, our first customers certainly made up for in enthusiasm and creativity. But if we were ever going to grow, we needed to cover more territory. For the first year or two of our existence, our brand's fame was limited mostly to certain elite circles on the West Coast. They were important to us as influencers and would help through much of the 1990s as we devoted our energies to establishing Patrón in the national marketplace. But there was still plenty of room to grow, so years later we applied a similar strategy to create visibility in more international markets.

Dick played his part in putting Patrón on the global glitterati map by thrusting a bottle into the hands of every star on every yacht and red carpet at the Cannes Film Festival. Suddenly, a bottle of Patrón became an automatic invitation to every A-list event on both sides of the ocean. One of his dear friends, Dyanne Fries, the daughter of the film and television producer Chuck Fries, just so happened to own a company, FMPC, that produced and set up booths for her clients at film festivals worldwide, including the Cannes Film Festival. On this particular trip, Dyanne was producing daily television spots about the goings-on at the festival that would air on huge video displays up and down La Croissette. The show was also streamed to television stations around the world. She needed help and invited Dick along to aid with the interviews with the understanding that he could promote some of his projects while there. Three days before the festival started, Dick had an idea for Patrón. He called Martin from France asking to be retained again and to please send cases of Patrón. Thus the guerrilla marketing games began anew in Europe.

Not generally known as an early riser, Dick got up early each morning to assist Dyanne in securing and producing movie star interviews that took place on various yachts, in hotels, and at premiere parties. Whether it was Michelle Yeoh or Jean-Claude Van Damme, the camera would not be turned on until Dick handed the star a bottle. This continued for two and a half weeks.

No opportunity was wasted. Because Dyanne was in charge, Dick waltzed into every event whether he was officially invited or not. He walked up to Jack Gilardi, the legendary Hollywood talent agent, and said: "I hear ICM's having a nightly party on the rooftop of the Noga Hilton. Want some Patrón?"

"Yeah!" came the inevitable reply.

Dick crashed the *InStyle* party at the famed Hotel du Cap, pulling up in a minivan filled with cases of Patrón and a camera crew, which was strictly forbidden at the famed hotel. The dumbfounded editor in chief of *InStyle* magazine told him, "This is a Veuve Cliquot party."

"Not anymore," said Dick, who had the hotel's general manager in tow. Dick had contacted him hours before asking if he carried Patrón in the hotel. The answer was no, but this lovely man also admitted he loved the brand and wanted it on the premises. "Let me make your day. If you make room for us, front and center, at the *In-Style* party, I will give you some cases to get you started," Dick said. "Done," the GM replied. These sponsored parties cost liquor suppliers a fortune, and the fact that Patrón opened the doors so easily revealed the intensity of the pent-up demand for it on the Continent.

By the end of the second day, every top hotel and bar in Cannes was stocked with Patrón, as were many of the major yachts. Word was beginning to spread. Dick would deliver a case to the yachts that hosted Dyanne's interviews as a thank you and casually approach those nearby, asking, "Permission to board? I have a gift." Whoever was hosting the yacht would reply, "You've got Patrón? Welcome aboard!" By then, Dick was becoming known on the Cannes scene, and so was Patrón. The international jet set was clamoring for a taste of this tequila they'd heard of, and now everyone was talking about it. Dick even made it onto the largest yacht in the world at the time. He had to take a tender to it, but the skipper was delighted to help when he saw the gift of Patrón he was carrying. There was so much talk about our brand at Cannes, you'd think Dick was handing out free Cartier bracelets.

THE MANSION

Back in Los Angeles, Martin and I became a regular presence at more of Hollywood's glamfests, often, but not always, alongside John Paul and Eloise. Our involvement with *Playboy*, for example, was a result of us choosing to use Playmates in our first fully paid print ads and sheer will on Martin's part. It paid off. Our relationship helped propel Patrón's national exposure even further.

Over the course of doing business with them, we became friendly with a few key members of the Playboy family: Cindy Rakowitz, head of Playboy promotions; and Denise and Gregg Schipper, who handled advertising and ad placements for the magazine, all of whom had dinner with us on numerous occasions. Denise and Cindy invited us to several events at the mansion, including the Midsummer Night's Dream Party and the New Year's Eve Party. We always went, as they were among the most buzzed about parties in Hollywood. We were always welcome, because people loved meeting the owner of Patrón.

But these parties were also strange affairs. Contrary to popular myth, there was no sex going on in the Grotto, at least not that I was aware of. No one was allowed to pick up a Bunny and go upstairs in the house for a midnight tryst. It was actually quite tame, considering. The usual suspects, rock 'n' rollers like Gene Simmons, male stars who considered themselves players like Scott Baio, came to gawk. There were also a few starlets who were trying too hard to be sexy—eye candy to fill the place. But everyone seemed somehow separate. No one was working the party. It was almost voyeuristic the way all the guests seemed to be on the outside, looking in on Hugh Hefner's storied lifestyle. The only people who seemed to be truly enjoying themselves were the six girlfriends Hef had at the time and all the other Playboy girls who were there to serve drinks and entertain the guests.

I've been to better raves. The food was mediocre, the grounds were just okay, and the pool area toilets were an overflowing mess. But as ambassadors for Patrón, it was necessary for us to see and be seen at the Playboy Mansion, and it wasn't terrible. We hung out with the inner circle: Denise, Gregg, Cindy, and all those who had to deliver something for the magazine. We most enjoyed talking to the girls serving drinks, who were down to earth, sweet, and above all, professional. They were wearing little else but skimpy lingerie or body paint, and were trained in comportment, so they had a certain grace. They were ladylike, careful to keep their legs together, their backs straight and always serving drinks from the side. Playboy has very strict rules about how its girls conduct themselves, and they understood the fine line between sexy and trashy. They were exactly the same principles that guided our Patrón Girls. In fact, the model we hired to be in our first ad campaign was the gorgeous Karen McDougal, 1998 Playmate of the Year.

MAKING AN ENTRANCE

Another memorable Hollywood event featuring our brand was the opening of Sir Richard Branson's Virgin megastore in Los Angeles. We'd been introduced to him in San Francisco through a mutual friend, Ian Duffel, a longtime executive at Virgin who believed both Martin and Sir Richard would benefit from the meeting. One of Martin's many dreams was to create a Patrón airline, a luxury private plane for hire emblazoned with Patrón branding. It was just another extension of his designer's disease. He even had a model airplane in our signature green with an image of the Patrón bee on its tail. Therefore, he was excited to meet the man who had created his own fleet. Sir Richard, meanwhile, was interested in launching a Virgin vodka and wanted to pick Martin's brain. In the end, neither discussion went anywhere, but Martin did agree to provide Patrón for Sir Richard's national debut in Los Angeles.

The megastore, which is now closed, was a round building with a courtyard on Sunset Boulevard, at the same address as the legendary Schwab's drugstore. Our party was in the courtyard, where we had created an elegant setup, with Patrón ice bars and Patrón Girls working the event. Live music and celebrity guests filled the space, but we were all anticipating the arrival of Sir Richard, who likes to make an entrance. This time, he opted for a swashbuckling theme and set up a zip line from the roof that would land him in the middle of the courtyard. Of course, it hadn't occurred to anyone that he would be landing in a space filled with people. As the daredevil business legend zoomed down the line, his dangling feet knocked into several elegantly coiffed heads. Fortunately, no one was hurt, but Sir Richard's face was beet red either from exertion or from embarrassment, I am not sure which. It was hysterical.

We saw him a few times after that in various locations around the world. Martin had great respect for Sir Richard. He saw in him the successful consumer brand mogul he aspired to be. But I simply enjoyed his company. He is a true character. What you see is what you get, with no airs. And he loves the ladies, especially our Patrón Girls.

BRAND AMBASSADORS

In addition to these lavish events, we made a point of using every opportunity large and small to promote Patrón. No other liquor brand on the market had a live person behind its name. Most were brands built long ago, with original founders who no longer had any connection to the product, or simply manufactured for today's market with no personal story behind them. But the Patrón story was unfolding as we built the business from scratch, and Martin was its protagonist. He made himself accessible to everyone as the discoverer and cofounder of the brand. Wherever we were, at a Hollywood party or in a restaurant, a bar, or even a supermarket, he was thrilled to sign bottles and shake the hands of Patrón's everyday consumers, as was John Paul.

That was why we took our own entertaining seriously indeed, particularly when we were hosting parties from home. JP, Eloise,

Martin, and I each had a role to play in representing the brand that involved creating an atmosphere of celebration, spontaneity, and fun. No detail was too small, and we prided ourselves on creating memorable experiences that were fueled by Patrón in the form of innovative cocktails and recipes infused with the spirit. Anyone leaving our home had to go away with the happiest of associations and sensory memories of our delicious brand. This, too, was business.

Because of the example we set, it was well understood by everyone around us what it meant to live the Patrón lifestyle. We had established a standard of behavior. John Paul reminded me of this fact recently when he described one of the earliest Patrón parties at his house in Beverly Hills.

It was late on a Sunday afternoon in 1990, and the empties of Patrón Tequila were piling up. About a hundred people, including celebrity and civilian friends, were gathered poolside, grooving to the Red Devils blues band while the last rays of sun bathed the backyard scene in golden light. The blues icon Johnny Rivers brought his guitar and couldn't resist jamming with the band, belting out all the classics: "Secret Agent Man," "The Poor Side of Town," "Memphis."

Cheech Marin was there, along with JP's neighbor from down the hill, James Woods, and his dear friend David Carradine, who drank a little extra that day. There was also a man nobody knew. Whoever brought him, he was more than welcome until something strange happened. David put his arm around the stranger and jumped in the pool fully clothed, dragging him along into the water. David was laughing, but the sopping wet gate crasher was not amused. In fact, he was furious and soon left the scene.

When David finally climbed out of the pool, JP asked him: "Who was that guy?"

"I have no idea, but he walked up to me, put his hand in his pocket, and pulled out a sheet of acid. He wanted us all tripping on LSD!"

David went on to explain to JP how he pulled the man into the pool to neutralize the acid. He knew it wasn't that kind of party. Our Patrón get-togethers were always about good times, laughter, and love. People got high, but it was a safe and clean high fueled by the purest tequila in the world. This was about living well and treating yourself to the best.

"JP, there was no way I was going to let this guy pass out acid at your party," David explained. "I knew you wouldn't stand for it, but I didn't want to disturb you, so I took the matter into my own hands."

Through Patrón, we had created a culture of refinement, good taste, and dedication to the finest things in life. We had established a creed that friends and fans of Patrón appreciated and lived by.

Of course, the DeJorias always managed to outdo us with their extravagance. Their home in Malibu was the scene of so many incredible celebrations, from their wedding reception, which even Cher attended, to some of the most decadent costume parties I have ever witnessed. One of their Christmas parties had a masquerade Renaissance theme, and when brass trumpeters announced our arrival, it felt like we were stepping onto the set for a movie about Henry VIII.

The ability to put on a memorable show was something the four of us shared. Although we could never compete with the spectacle, Martin and I stepped up our entertaining when we moved to Montecito, making up in creativity and sensuality what we lacked in budget. Week after week, we were either part of a crowd or entertaining a crowd. We were determined to spread the love of this amazing brand Martin had discovered and developed. We got up-close and personal, making sure Patrón was on the lips of everyone with whom we came in contact. Just as well, as we were extremely social creatures.

Such was life in those early years of Patrón: a blur of parties. It was all work and all play, and I relished every single moment.

CHAPTER 5

By the Seat of Our Pants

S ERENDIPITY SURROUNDED us those first few years with Patrón. Somehow, being open to everything and having no set course or agenda had created moments of magic that came to define who we were as a brand. In fact, Martin would never have discovered Patrón if he had not been completely in the moment the day he was driving through the hills of Jalisco. It was as if the universe were giving these little gifts to let us know we were on the right path.

Early on, within the first few months of starting the business, Martin and I chartered a yacht and set sail in the Caribbean with a few friends: Tom and Caroline Law and Gregg Gann and his then wife, Monette. We sailed from St. Maarten to Grenada, anchoring at many of the islands en route. We had no itinerary or schedule, just three happy couples feeling totally free, sharing their mutual passion for sailing the seas, fraternizing with the islanders, and experiencing their diverse cultures. High on life and Patrón, skinny-dipping, and catching fish along the way, we headed south, making quite an impression at each port of call. We were making margaritas as we approached Grenada. While emptying a Patrón bottle, Martin got the notion to write a note, place it in the bottle, and throw it out to sea just for the fun of it, so we did. Martin wrote on the back of one of his business cards: "Whoever finds this bottle will receive a case of Patrón tequila with my compliments. Please call."

We corked the bottle, taped and sealed it securely, and tossed it overboard. It was a poetic gesture. The bottle even looked like it belonged at sea, bobbing out of sight. Why not?

Two years later, working at his desk in Montecito, Martin got a call from a young woman.

"I found a bottle with your card in it," she said.

"Excuse me? What are you talking about?" Martin asked. By then he'd completely forgotten what we'd done.

"Last week my husband and I were in Bermuda on our honeymoon, walking along the beach, when we saw something shining in the sand."

They dug it up, uncorked the bottle, and found Martin's card in pristine condition. How the current could have carried it all the way there was a mystery.

We were thrilled and of course Martin honored his promise and sent them a case of Patrón: the perfect wedding gift. The idea that our casual offering to the ocean could eventually find its way into the hands of a deserving pair of newlyweds still gives me goose bumps.

UNCHARTED WATERS

If only it were always that simple, but it's never smooth sailing when you're starting a new business in an industry that is completely unfamiliar. There were plenty of white knuckle moments. Early on there were some critical mistakes made, and production and distribution snafus were a constant concern. While luck played a part in the early days with marketing and getting the brand on the lips of Hollywood's biggest tastemakers, building a following did not happen overnight.

Part of our challenge was that a market for ultrapremium tequila simply did not exist in the late 1980s and early 1990s. There was no precedent. In those days, people drank mostly vodka, wine, and beer, and in very unimaginative ways. Mixed drinks consisted of two ingredients at most. People were more likely to order vodka mixed with tonic or orange juice than a martini. A gin and tonic or Scotch and soda were about as exotic as you could get.

Even the ubiquitous Cosmo had not yet appeared on the bar scene. In fact, there was no cocktail scene. Those fabulous days of inventive post-Prohibition drinks such as the sidecar, the old fashioned, the pink squirrel, and the gin fizz had petered out by the 1960s. Spirits were not glorified by hip young things the way they are now. Bartenders had not been elevated to the status of mixologists, and there was no pride in the quality of ingredients or the artful way a cocktail was put together. There were no fancy glasses or inventive names. Even drinking and collecting fine wine was not common. There simply wasn't a level of appreciation for quality in the wine and spirits industry. There was no consciousness about spirits or wines, and people didn't really care what they drank. If anything, alcohol was considered a guilty pleasure, consumed purely for the high and not the taste. People didn't know better, so they accepted the notion that liquor wasn't supposed to taste good. It was a means to a feel-good end in a decadent time when people were experimenting with all kinds of substances.

We had our work cut out for us reeducating the public about quality and conscious consumption. But that was just one piece of a large and complex puzzle. Not only were we faced with having to reinvent the cocktail culture, we had to figure out the basics of a business that involved many aspects of production, packaging, shipping, and distribution. A steep learning curve had to be surmounted when it came to the operations side of the business, and we often bumped up against harsh realities.

It was a lengthy nightmare fine-tuning the bottles. Because they were handblown, the diameter of the bottle necks varied to such a degree that the only solution was to inventory six different-size corks. Meeting the standards of the Bureau of Alcohol, Tobacco, and Firearms (ATF) was another major production problem. Again, the handblown individual works of art factor contributed to slight size variances, which resulted in some bottles appearing to hold less volume than others. Inspectors held up shipments and investigations ensued until finally the ATF conceded that all the bottles, regardless of how they appeared, correctly contained the required 750 milliliters of liquid. But that recovery was short-lived. Subsequently we were informed of, and forced to comply with, the prescribed minimum amount of air space required between the bottom of the cork and the liquor in each bottle, thus allowing for expansion in changing climate conditions. If this minimum was not strictly adhered to, the contents might have blown. The issue wasn't resolved for several months, until Martin introduced molds in the glassblowing process to standardize sizes.

Sourcing all the different materials for packaging was a vast logistical undertaking. There were many different components to the packaging: corks, ribbon, a booklet, five labels, tissue paper, shrink-wrap, and the boxes. The corks ultimately came from Portugal, and the boxes, ribbons, and paper mostly from the United States but also from other parts of the world, so there were global shipping costs to boot.

Although most weren't aware of the extent of his generosity, Martin rewarded his staff handsomely and would give everyone at

Patrón a handsome bonus each Christmas. But when it came to suppliers, he was hell-bent on paying as little as possible and was a master at hammering the price down. As any businessperson knows, every penny saved per item adds up and increases profit margins, especially when there are so many components involved in production and packaging.

Every time there was a design change, it took numerous costly and wasteful production runs to get it right. First, the Moorish-looking glass ball on top of each bottle had a glass stem that went into the top of the cork and was held there with an adhesive. But finding glue that had the approval of the U.S. Food and Drug Administration (FDA) and didn't break down from the alcohol was next to impossible. Upon opening, the glass stopper would pull out of the cork, leaving it stuck in the bottle's neck. Attempts were made to educate the front line to "rock" the stopper cork out as opposed to pulling it, but that proved unsuccessful. Martin finally had to ditch the beautiful glass stopper design and mimic the look by using all-cork stoppers.

"PRACTICE POPULATION"

The packaging was evolving by trial and error. Adding to these challenges was the fact that the glass factory was at a separate location, far from the tequila factory. The constant frustrations became a source of much dinner-table conversation, and Gregg, our sailing friend, would always joke with Martin about the pitfalls of conducting business in Mexico. The two met through JP soon after APM began. Martin sourced some Mexican ceramic tiles for Gregg, who was remodeling some properties in his portfolio. Gregg had once owned a business that imported goods from Mexico, including handblown glass, and warned Martin that quality could be inconsistent at best when one was manufacturing south of the border. He was both amused by and sympathetic to what Martin was up against. The challenges of getting things done in Mexico were notorious.

"The problem with Mexico is that it is a practice population," Martin would say on his most frustrating days. But John Paul disagreed, as he only had positive experiences with the Mexican people.

Hiccups began immediately. The production deal almost fell apart just days after the factory received the signed contract. Randomly, some clause was deemed unfair, and attorneys from both sides had to meet again in person and go through each term line by line with a translator. Martin had to fly down to the factory, show his face, and patiently explain to them yet again that he only wanted what was fair for both sides. He did not do business any other way.

It was a case of constantly putting out fires. Production stopped on a whim. Whether it was for a family function, a birthday, a holy day, or simply because someone was mad at Martin, work would slow down with unpredictable frequency.

It was then we realized that we had to expect problems all the way down the line and be as flexible as possible in dealing with them, addressing each issue as it arose. We could not assume that someone else would take care of it. Of course, Martin had Francisco to help him, but the fact that Martin owned the brand did not mean he was above staying in the trenches even as the business was growing. Often, Martin would have to fly down because a piece of equipment wasn't working or something was wrong with a batch. He and Francisco would have to go through every detail of the process to troubleshoot until things were up and running again.

We supplied all the packaging materials in quantities commensurate with production forecasts. When shipments were delayed because of inexplicable depletions of one thing or another, Martin was exasperated.

"You shouldn't be out. Why didn't you tell me you were getting low?" he would invariably ask them.

No answers.

The extent of the delays depended on which item was missing. Tissue paper for the boxes or ribbon could be brought in within a day or two, but labels, booklets, and boxes were all printed components that required more time.

The family who owned the factory that originally made Patrón were extremely proud. Before we came along, they only had one Japanese customer, yet they already lived well. Then Martin and John Paul came into their lives, and that deal made them wealthy beyond anything they'd ever experienced. They recognized and embraced the joint accomplishment and were usually receptive and responsive to suggestions for growth, but they lacked the entrepreneurial fire that defined who Martin was. Naturally, it led to some significant cultural and personality clashes.

TEQUILA TANTRUMS

Other than Francisco and one woman whom we'll call Maria, an assistant in the factory offices, no one there spoke English. We were never quite sure what was being translated, but poor communication often led to a breakdown in diplomatic relations. On one occasion, when Martin learned that production had stopped because one owner had been fighting with his wife and was too upset to work, he momentarily lost his cool, which didn't help. It wasn't in his heart to show anyone disrespect or treat people unfairly, but for the first couple of years they didn't know his heart. They eventually got used to his forthright manner, but it took a while, and another owner was particularly untrusting in the beginning.

Her insistence on doing everything her way exacerbated the problems between Los Angeles and Jalisco. There were numerous little tantrums. A few times shipments would be halted from delivery to the United States because Martin had unintentionally upset the family. He was only trying to make things more efficient for everyone, but any suggestion was received as an insult. When shipments finally did get on their way to the U.S. border, bandits often hijacked the trucks. It was a rare occurrence when a shipment arrived without at least a few bottles missing.

It should have been simple. Only a certain number of bottles could fit in cases and be packed in each truck. When shipping documents arrived, we should have been able to issue payments with our eyes closed. But that was never the case. As a result, we simply could not keep up with demand in those early years.

ABLE ALLY

One of Martin's most brilliant decisions was to put Francisco on our payroll within months of launching Patrón. Francisco was not a relative of the factory owners and was always treated as something of an outsider even though his genius contributed to the greatness of Patrón. He oversaw everything, from the agave fields, where he consulted with the *jimadores* on the readiness of the harvest, to the distillation process and the bottling, ensuring that nothing would compromise the quality and taste of each batch. Yet he wasn't paid adequately and was treated by the family owners with little respect.

By hiring Francisco at a much higher salary and giving him the deserved title "Master Distiller," Martin could ensure that he had his own man on the ground so that there would be no shortcuts or shenanigans as the factory expanded and increased production.

Although it meant one fewer person for them to pay, the owners deeply resented Francisco for changing teams and treated him like a spy from the enemy camp. The poor man endured their derision and abuse for years. This gentle, respectful, and kind soul didn't deserve the ill treatment. He was largely responsible for creating the great tequila that became Patrón, and without him they would not have had such a successful business. But Martin made it well worth his while.

Francisco is a scientist who knows tequila production like no other, so having him on board was critical. His impeccable taste buds contributed to the development and launch of Patrón XO Cafe, a coffee tequila, in 1992, and Citronge Orange Liqueur a year later. Flavored tequilas were unique in the marketplace, so it was a big risk. In fact, this was many years before any spirit category, including vodka, began introducing flavor infusions. But developing these variations on the original was no simple task. Our new products had to be exquisite in keeping with the clean, pure taste that Patrón was known for, not syrupy and sickly sweet. Martin and Francisco pulled it off, conjuring up raves from beverage reviewers.

Patrón XO Cafe has a bold, full-bodied espresso flavor, with a Patrón Silver base that gives it dryness, and is 70 proof. Citronge is bright and crisp with no artificial flavors or colors. Although both of these have not reached the level of the straight tequilas, they have broadened the customer base and sales have been steady. Of course, creating new bottles, packaging, and product compounded the logistic nightmares, as they were all made in different factories.

SHELF LIFE

Mexico wasn't the only source of tension on this white knuckle ride. The right distribution infrastructure can make or break a spirit brand.

If you don't have an enthusiastic and knowledgeable sales force in large enough numbers to give you national coverage, you will soon disappear from the shelves. It is everything.

At first, Wine Warehouse was the perfect fit for us. It was small, which meant that an emerging brand such as Patrón would not get lost in the crowd. But it distributed solely in California. After the first year, we outgrew them.

There are two tiers of distributors in the liquor industry. The top tier is made up of large national distributors such as Diageo, Jim Beam, and, at that time, Seagram's. The second tier consists of regional distributors who are contracted by those "master" distributors to sell various brands to all the bars, restaurants, liquor stores, duty-free stores, and grocery stores. These more localized distributors include the likes of Southern Wine & Spirits and Young's Market Company, which are large companies in and of themselves, with sales offices all over the country.

But the usual goal is to get a distribution deal with one of the big, top-tier companies, which buy the brand in bulk, warehouse it, and ship it out to the various second-tier distributors in each state. With these master distributors, a spirit brand has only one accounts receivable, and they in turn contract out to several second-tier sales and distribution companies to manage the thousands of retail customers purchasing a brand all over the country; this eliminates a huge headache on the operations and accounting side for the brand owners.

The other huge advantage is that the bigger the distribution company, the greater the national and international coverage and the deeper the pockets for investment in things such as marketing campaigns and promotional events. That's why the goal with any burgeoning brand is to graduate to a bigger and bigger top-tier master distributor each time.

BOOTS ON THE GROUND

After Wine Warehouse, we signed with Jim Beam. It was the first time Patrón went national. Finally we had an army of salespeople to educate, so it wasn't just Martin, JP, and I doing it by ourselves, although it was extraordinary what we could achieve with such a small team.

Martin had one assistant from the beginning. Over the next few years, he slowly added two gentlemen to oversee sales: Ed Blinn and Burt Stewart. There was nothing corporate about Patrón. It doesn't take a lot of bodies to build a vibrant and successful business, just the right combination of a great product, people, an irrepressible entrepreneurial spirit, and enthusiasm. Being small and nimble worked in those days. All energy could go into running the business as opposed to running the staff. We were always methodical and in the moment, and getting it done was truly enjoyable for us.

Patrón infused everything we did, whether it was socializing with friends or indulging in our many recreational interests. Celebrities were by no means our first or only avenues of brand exposure. By talking about the brand and living the lifestyle, we became associated with it, and our friends and acquaintances soon caught the bug. Everywhere we went we introduced ourselves as Patrón brand ambassadors, to the point where even the guys at the valet service desks knew our car and the fact that it belonged to "the owners of Patrón."

This created a ripple effect. One friend tells 10 friends, and each of those friends tells 10 more. We'd soon created an entire network of friends and acquaintances two or three times removed and instructed them to please ask for Patrón wherever they went—liquor and grocery stores, bars and restaurants, airport duty-free shops— even when we knew they were living in states where we did not yet have distribution. If three people asked for Patrón at any establishment, management would remember and seek out our product on its next purchase orders. It was what we called "pulling from the front." One by one, 10 by 10, and 20 by 20, we were steadily creating an enormous energy flow that was fueling demand, and it was a thrill. There is nothing like standing in a bar and hearing some stranger order your brand. Even now, without a stake in the business, I feel a rush each time someone asks for Patrón by name.

WALKING BILLBOARDS

We didn't just talk about Patrón, we advertised it wherever we went and made a point of donning our own swag every time we traveled for events or conventions across the country and around the world. Martin would wear a Patrón T-shirt or sweatshirt, and I would wear our ladies baby T and yoga pants emblazoned with our branding. I also carried our "Patrón planet saver" bag. The point was that every time we passed through an airport, thousands of pairs of eyes would see us. Every time we flew to Anguilla, we had to change planes in Miami or New York, so we had to represent the brand. It didn't matter if Patrón wasn't sold in those cities. We had to imprint Patrón on people's minds; it's all about images.

It's why we had a very specific approach to Patrón swag. We needed both men and women to actually wear it out. All the spirit brands had baseball caps and T-shirts, but ours were not the baggy, shapeless kind that gets thrown in the bottom of the drawer. They were fashionable. It's always easy to get men to throw on a branded T or hat, but we deliberately designed our women's wear to be sexy and trendy, something a woman would actually want to put on when she went out for errands or a drink with her friends. In the early 1990s, the style was baby T-shirts that barely covered the midriff and cap sleeves with ruffles. We also had yoga pants before they were called yoga pants, with heart-shaped logos emblazoned on the tush. The women's Patrón caps were more like sleek cycling hats in keeping with a feminine style. Many times I was stopped in the street or at an airport terminal and asked where I got my outfit.

The thinking was that people would rather look at what a woman is wearing than at a man's clothing. The eye will always be drawn to a pretty girl in a tight T-shirt, and everyone will take note of a logo that's flashed across a nice pair of breasts. When a man and a woman walk into a room together, people always look at the woman first. Even women check out women first. Why not exploit that fact for the sake of branding? No one else was doing it, then or now.

Of course, we couldn't always be in complete control of how our message was conveyed. By now our promotional events were taking place at locations across the United States as well as the Caribbean and, to some extent, Europe. We usually had two Patrón Girls working each promotional event in bars and restaurants who required close monitoring. That little dress I had put together with my tailor was now being manufactured, and we were buying 60 at a time to send all over the country for various events. People were trying to buy it off the Patrón Girls' backs.

We attempted to maintain the fine line between the girls looking chic sexy rather than cheap. On one occasion, at an event, I had to pull a young lady into the bathroom to literally clean her up. Her streetwalker makeup, wild uncombed hair, foul mouth, and mud-encrusted stilettos were unacceptable. While I redid her face, styled her hair, and cleaned off her shoes, I was coaching her on her general conduct and how to speak professionally. She actually appreciated the makeover, as I was viewed as one of the girls. No one seemed to take offense, and luckily, the lack of close monitoring of out-of-town events never seemed to backfire on us. We had an image to uphold, and in those early days we had to build a presence, which meant never straying from our standards and maintaining the Patrón way.

With more salespeople dedicated to our brand who were growing increasingly familiar with our unconventional approach, we were gaining more control over how we were represented across the country. Additional boots on the ground saved us in many ways. When a sales rep called JP from Chicago to let him know that a liquor store was selling Patrón at a discount, we were able to take immediate action and buy every bottle that store had in stock. Thankfully, it was a new market that had yet to be fully educated, so it was natural that the product was slow to move, but the last thing we wanted was to be seen in some fire sale. It was the first and final time that ever happened in the history of Patrón.

UNIQUE LOGIC

We devised our own way of motivating the distributors to pay special attention to Patrón above all competing brands. Some had at least 30 other products to sell. Martin structured the price of our products so that they would make a much larger profit compared with other brands. It was a decision he made not on the basis of experience but from sheer logic and necessity. We had to do all we could to get noticed. By the end of each year, the greater profit margin was obvious. They might not have sold as many bottles of Patrón as bottles of the other brands, but they sure as hell made more money incrementally than they did on anyone else's products. It's not hard to understand why Patrón became their brand of choice.

We didn't know how it was done in the business. We were flying by the seat of our pants and imagining how it *should* be done. We were fairly intelligent people with business sense and a lot of creativity.

We thought we'd figured out the most logical route, only to learn that was never the way it was actually done. For the most part, by not knowing any better, we actually *did* better. We weren't boxing ourselves in with a certain standard. We didn't even know what the box was! At the same time, we weren't trying to be different. We were simply trying to do the best we could with what we had.

One of the biggest barriers to entry for a new liquor product is getting on the retailer's shelves. If no one knows you and you don't already have a customer following, there is absolutely no incentive for a store owner to give up precious shelf real estate that might otherwise be occupied by a product with proven sales. Connecting with Steve Wallace at Wally's was one of our first lucky breaks on that front, because he specialized in luxury brands and had an interest in presenting something exciting, unique, and expensive to his customers, who included some of the biggest names in Hollywood. Steve already sold a tequila he felt was of high quality and had been a tequila drinker himself for years, but when Martin administered the taste test, he was instantly won over. Moreover, our packaging matched the quality of our fine product, whereas the tequila that Wally's carried was contained in a rather ordinary bottle. It wasn't long before Patrón displaced the other brand on Wally's shelves.

Grassroots marketing and the fostering of a personal relationship with Steve, who became our friend and a regular at our parties, got us in the right place at the right time. Wally's was perfect placement for us not only because of its association with luxury but because this retailer set the trends. Dozens of other restaurants and outlets subscribed to Wally's newsletter in order to understand what was hot and desirable in the marketplace, so our presence in the store had an impact that went far beyond that one retail channel. Even celebrities and publicists read Wally's newsletter to be in the know about what to consume or send out as gifts.

Individual relationships such as the one we cultivated with Steve meant everything to our success. Motivating our front lines was critical. Equally important if not more important are the people who come into direct contact with the end customer. In our case, that included bartenders, wait staff, restaurateurs, and retailers. It ensured that we were remembered.

Within months, the entire Los Angeles area knew that we were associated with Patrón, which was unique in an industry in which there is rarely a live person behind the brand. It's what the best salespeople do: build personal relationships.

JP excelled at this in his other business, JPMS, constantly having events for thousands of hairdressers from around the globe. He knew how to make the people who were his first point of sales feel important and valued. We did the same for our front line and sales force with parties and various promotions. One of our tactics was to have incentive programs for bartenders. Other companies usually offered programs to the sales force, which we also did, but never the bar staff. In one, Martin spiffed bartenders $25 for every Patrón cork they turned in, and we received bags full of corks.

FRUIT-INFUSED PROMOTION

We were constantly coming up with new ways to stir excitement on the bar scene. One evening, while we were lounging on the beach in Marina del Rey with our friends Tom and Caroline Law, Martin came up with the most divine concoction. He found a big bell jar and began to layer thick slices of watermelon, pineapple, mango, and fresh ginger until the jar was full. Then he poured three bottles of Patrón Silver and one of Citronge Orange Liqueur over the fruit mixture.

He let it sit like that for a while. The jar had a spigot at the bottom, and what came out tasted like heaven, with no alcohol flavor whatsoever. It was a slam dunk. Immediately Martin started trying to sort out how this could become a "program" for bars and restaurants, and we began fantasizing and brainstorming what it could be called. I came up with the name FIP (Fruit Infused Patrón), and that was the one that stuck.

Right there on the beach, another marketing campaign was born, and bar and restaurant accounts loved it. Our warehouse wasn't exactly equipped for food preparation, but we went ahead and hired a couple of people to peel and slice the fruit, filling up hundreds of bell jars to ship out to establishments all over Los Angeles. The deal was that we would supply them with the fruit-filled jar, and they would have to commit to a certain amount of product to make the cocktail. Of course, they loved FIP not only for its fabulous taste but because it was a big moneymaker. Although four bottles of liquor were used, it produced six to eight bottles of the liquid because of the juice from the fruit. The jars emptied out fast, and because the fruit was compressing and liquefying, they would fill up again after about an hour. We only supplied the first jar of fruit; after that, the bars and restaurants prepared FIP in their own kitchens.

No other brand would have considered doing something like this. It was a huge hit and got people to taste and appreciate Patrón who might otherwise have been afraid of tequila and introduced consumers to Citronge, not to mention the fact that it looked beautiful on bar tops. From a business perspective, however, we were being green. We realized during the six months the program ran that we had to monitor the end users closely. It was a huge headache. In some establishments, we found a jar with just a few pieces of pineapple floating inside. Others took our jars and replaced Patrón with vodka. We couldn't have our name on that.

At one point, we thought about bottling FIP, but we simply didn't have the infrastructure at the time, even though we did have a name, Patrón Pleaser.

SETTING SAIL

Another early example of Patrón promotion was an international yacht race we entered in 1991. Again, we were living it, co-opting our personal passions to promote Patrón, whether it was yachting, polo, or in my case, Latin dancing. Before I knew him, Martin had owned a yacht that he raced around the world, so when it was time for the annual Newport to Ensenada event, we decided to charter a sailboat called *Taxi Dancer*. The 24-hour race that finishes in the Mexican port town was an international media event that was broadcast everywhere, so it was the perfect way to get our brand on the small screen and in all the newspapers and sporting magazines.

The event took place in April, the day after the Rodney King beating, when riots were breaking out all over Los Angeles. The city was in a virtual lockdown. As we drove down to Newport just a few hours before our kickoff party the night before the race began, we saw dozens of National Guard Hummers driving in the other direction along the freeway. We were thrilled to be getting out of town.

Martin bought and customized a spinnaker—that huge sail at the front of the boat—with the Patrón colors and logo. The spinnaker is the sail that's always used in the morning to catch the most breeze, when we were most likely to be seen by all the camera crews at the start of the race, many of which were flying above us in helicopters. We had Patrón Girls on board, so our boat and crew were sufficiently photogenic.

We did poorly in the race. We couldn't catch a good wind and got off course. It was boring, drifting along day and night without ever picking up much speed. There was little else to do but eat and drink. But as far as international press attention went, it was mission accomplished.

Sometimes our brilliant ideas came back to bite us in the face. We launched a six-month program for the distributor's sales force in which the one who sold the most Patrón would win a customized Harley-Davidson bike complete with the green and black Patrón detailing. But by the time the contest was over, we were advised by Seagram's, Patrón's distributor at the time, that it was too much of a liability to give a motorcycle away. If the winner was hurt or killed while riding it, we'd be liable. It was ridiculous but true. We gave the victor the cash equivalent of the Harley instead, and the bike became one of JP's favorite toys.

MOMENTUM SHIFT

Overall, it was clear that most of these methods were working. You can tell when a brand is gaining real momentum simply by being out there in the world. Every time Martin, JP, or I went to a restaurant or a bar, we'd order Patrón Tequila.

At first, the answer would be, "What tequila?" Then, what felt like a couple of months later, the waiter or bartender would invariably say, "Let me check." By the end of the first year and a half, they would reply, "Would you like Silver or Gold?"

It took us a few years to go national, but by liquor industry standards it was a rocket ship ride. At first, bars would put in orders for only one or two bottles; then orders grew to a case and then to several cases. When that began to happen, the salespeople were like sharks that smell blood in the water, and they started pushing Patrón even more aggressively. They knew they were on to a winner.

By 1994, we had outgrown Jim Beam. They told Martin and JP that because we were "too high-end," the most they could ever sell of Patrón was 20,000 cases a year, even though we were already on target to exceed that number—a major disconnect. It was a clear signal that Jim Beam did not share our vision for the brand, and so they were dropped. We had already defied the expectations of the market, so why accept the limits of what I thought was a dusty old corporation completely lacking in imagination?

Of course, it's never a perfectly seamless transition from one top-tier distributor to the next. There are often gaps in between. Fortunately, Martin and JP had by then established a connection with Southern Wine & Spirits, one of the biggest second-tier distributors in the state. Southern worked closely with Seagram's in California and Florida, and Seagram's was the kind of top-tier corporate giant we hoped to move up to next.

TALL DARK STRANGER

Soon after we ended our relationship with Wine Warehouse and shortly before the relationship with Jim Beam, JP, with the stunning Eloise on his arm, had the foresight to pay a house call to the Los Angeles offices of Ted Simpkins, the managing director of Southern Wine & Spirits at that time. In an interview for this book, Ted recalled that first meeting in vivid detail. When you meet JP, his swashbuckling good looks are hard to forget. As he walked into the lobby, Ted's assistant, Nicky, wasn't quite sure what to make of him.

"Mr. Simpkins, there's a strange-looking fellow who wants to come and speak with you about tequila, but I'm not sure whether or not to let him upstairs," she told him, phoning up from the reception desk.

"Strange how?" he asked.

"Well, he has a long ponytail and he's dressed all in black. But he has a beautiful woman with him."

"Send him up," Ted said.

John Paul introduced himself and showed Ted a bottle that had a crooked label. It must have been from an older shipment, when we were still in the process of getting our packaging just right. But Ted hardly noticed. Eloise was sitting behind JP, to his right, and he couldn't take his eyes off her. JP, the sly fox, knew exactly what he was doing.

He began his pitch, enticing Ted to taste the contents of the slightly imperfect Patrón bottle, and of course Ted was duly impressed. Ted was a veteran who knew his business like no other, and he was aware the time was right for an ultrapremium tequila. He'd come across countless bartenders and mixologists who were interested in selling a high-end tequila. But he still had his doubts.

"You've got balls charging twice the price of any other tequila on the market," he told JP.

"Clint Eastwood drinks it," JP replied.

"Yes, but does he buy it?"

"Yes, he does."

Ted finally agreed to take it on. Southern was a growing and aggressive company at the time, and he liked Martin and JP's moxie and the fact that they were doing things differently. He also had a hunch that our higher price point meant he could make a bigger profit.

We had picked a perfect ally. Ted had been in liquor sales since 1971 and knew from experience what JP and Martin instinctively understood, that this was a business about relationships. Although large liquor companies frequently change leadership at the top, the sales reps in the trenches are almost always the same people.

"We are a C-student business," Ted still likes to say, and he means it as a compliment. In other words, whether the salespeople are calling on a French restaurant or a strip club, these accounts are usually self-made entrepreneurs who work 80 hours a week. They don't have Harvard MBAs or trust funds. More often, they are bartenders, sommeliers, restaurant managers, even cocktail waitresses who slogged for years and worked their way up the food chain. They, more than anyone, appreciate the personal touch of a rep who knows their story and has been doing business with them for years, and it's that relationship, more than any kind of expensive ad campaign, that is going to determine whether they are going to give a new product a shot in their establishment. It has been thus ever since Prohibition.

Martin and JP lived this ethos every day. JP built up his hair care business by personally getting to know the likes and dislikes of the hair salon owners and stylists who bought his products. Martin did the same with Patrón. We sold to individuals, not chains. As the cofounder of an increasingly popular brand, Martin was already becoming wealthy from his business, and JP was well known as a hair care mogul. But they were never above sitting down in a bar with their customers and having a drink. They made themselves accessible. That was unusual in a business where brands are usually owned by giant and impersonal corporations, and our distributors loved them for it.

TIME BOMB

Being among the customers took a tremendous amount of time and commitment and, in Martin's case, a health toll. His biggest secret was that he had a heart problem. He had many issues that would have caused most people to slow down and ease up on life's excesses, including the fact that he'd lost a kidney. But the cardiomyopathy was what made him a ticking time bomb. His heart muscles were weak. His heart was enlarged, and the valves didn't close completely, causing the blood to back up, which meant his heart wasn't able to pump adequate amounts through his body.

In the early days of our courtship, he hadn't deigned to tell me, but I found out after a few months when his heart went out of rhythm and had to be shocked back into a regular beat. Going through it with him the first time, put the fear of God in me. Losing this man, the love of my life, was something I just wasn't able to comprehend.

Pam, the friend who introduced us, filled me in, and I was furious at Martin for withholding the information from me. He'd been under strict doctor's orders to give up alcohol. After that first scare with me, he was good about the drinking. But it left us with a dilemma.

In the liquor industry, you need to be seen out there, enjoying your own product, but never too much. Moderation is essential. When he wasn't drinking, Martin and I worked out this pantomime where he would always allow someone to pour a drink for him. Discreetly swapping glasses, I would drink his or, if I had already had enough, pour it away when no one was looking. At our dinner parties, which always involved the most amazing wines, I was shuffling glasses all the time.

But the closet teetotaling never lasted for more than a few months. Working in the liquor industry, Martin was surrounded by far too much temptation. Of course he was going to give in to it, and before long his heart would go out of rhythm again. The additional stresses of a growing business did not help either.

THE BIG LEAGUES

When we were between first-tier distributors, we simply couldn't get Patrón out there on the shelves. By 1995, we had cases of Patrón piling up in our warehouse with nowhere to go. But because we'd promised to buy all of their production, we had to keep taking it regardless. It was costing us hundreds of thousands of dollars to carry this inventory with each passing month, and Patrón was drying up on the market. We needed the infrastructure and national sales coverage of a distribution giant, and the sooner the better.

Through Southern, we eventually forged a relationship with Seagram's, and by 1995 Martin was negotiating both a distribution deal and a partnership in building a tequila factory in Mexico. When Seagram's first expressed interest in signing a distribution deal with us, we were ecstatic.

At last, we thought, we made it to the big leagues.

The industry had gone through so much consolidation that there were only a couple of players left to work with, so when Seagram's finally reciprocated our interest, it seemed like a godsend. But our courtship was taking just a little too long. Contract negotiations were getting brutal, and after nine months of going back and forth, it's not like we had much choice. From the bars to the liquor stores, people were screaming for Patrón, and we had to get our product to them before all momentum was lost.

We were naive and underrepresented. We learned the hard way that when you sign a deal with a distributor, the minimums they commit to must include the amounts they will actually sell versus what they will buy. In so many ways, they had us over the proverbial barrel, and Martin, who was no pushover when it came to negotiating a deal, was outgunned.

Martin's heart condition was getting worse by the day, and I could tell that he was out of rhythm. The drinking had resumed, and the weight was piling on, contributing to his sleep apnea. Each night, I would fall asleep with my ear to his chest to make sure I could hear the steady thump, thump, thump and know he was all right. It was always a relief when he woke up the next morning.

And that was just the beginning of the heartache.

CHAPTER 6

The High Life

E VEN BEFORE OUR relationship with Seagram's started, Martin
and I were coming up in the world. After five years living together in Marina del Rey, we decided to upgrade to Windsong, our
stunning Montecito estate overlooking the Pacific. While still in Los
Angeles, Martin witnessed a drive-by shooting, and that was it. Besides, we could afford the upgrade. By that time Martin and JP had
grown Patrón into a multi-million-dollar business, with sales doubling
every year despite the many logistic challenges. We were definitely
starting to feel the ease of life.

At first the investment was something of a stretch for us. It was
1995, just a few short years after the birth of Patrón. It would be
months before we completed our negotiations with Seagram's and
cash would start to flow in any significant volume. But our dear friend
Warwick Miller gave us an initial loan, which we paid off within a
year, so that we could do all we needed to make Windsong ours.

It was perfect, because Warwick and his wife, our closest friends,
had their West Coast home nearby in Montecito at the time, so their
neighbors and acquaintances became ours, and vice versa. We didn't
have to start over entirely. We had a ready-made list of local dinner

guests. Sadly, the Millers moved back to Australia shortly afterward, although Warwick always stayed with us when he was passing through on his way to New York. There was always room at the inn.

As soon as we walked onto the estate, we felt the magic. It would serve both as our home and as Patrón's West Coast head office, the incubator where we would hatch our most ingenious plans for the brand. We couldn't think of a more perfect and inspiring epicenter. The business and lifestyle had become intertwined, and we were determined to make Windsong a kind of extension of the Patrón brand, a physical emblem of the way of life we stood for.

There was an indescribable energy to this property, which was set atop a hill with 180-degree views of the Pacific; it was the kind of view you hope to get during a stay at a six-star resort on the French Riviera. There was a koi pond with huge, gleaming carp of assorted colors that must have been worth a fortune. We had three spacious guesthouses, a pool, a lake, orchards, and gardens everywhere you looked. The property was spectacular in every respect, both inside and out.

Best of all was a vast greenhouse situated on a slope adjacent to the main house. When we bought the property, the greenhouse was something of a ruin, but Martin's imagination was on fire. He spent months designing and then renovating it into a magnificent showpiece. It was an office that felt nothing like one, full of lush tropical vegetation, with the soothing sound of running water from an indoor fish pond's waterfall. Sunlight poured into the glass and stone dwelling covered with a canvas roof. There were 18-inch-thick stone walls with magnificent round glass windows etched with the Patrón bee, a huge fireplace, thick foliage throughout, and panoramic views of the ocean. The koi pond complete with two stepping-stones provided passage from the reception, and the only route to Martin's area. It felt like a true Japanese Zen garden and housed Martin and his

Martin and I, as usual, being our affectionate selves
(mid- to late-1990s)

Martin and I chilling at home on the Marina Peninsula beach
(early 1990s)

One of the original Patrón girls, Heather, holding one of the original Patrón bottles with a glass stopper (early 1990s)

Two more of the original Patrón girls, Christine and me, with Martin at the Patrón sponsored Rodeo event (mid-1990s)

Martin and tequila master Francisco Alcaraz on the beach at our home in Anguilla, after a long day's work at the rum factory (mid- to late-1990s)

Me with John Paul DeJoria
and his wife, Eloise,
being escorted into the
Rodeo event at the Burbank
Equestrian Center
(mid-1990s)

Celebrity Sports
Invitational, Hawaii.
Patrón girls jet ski race
team, with Martin, JP, an
unidentified gentleman,
and me (1995)

MARTIN CROWLEY

Martin memorial photo—the
love of my life as his best self

JANUARY 29, 1943 - APRIL 19, 2003

Windsong, our Montecito home and Patrón's California head office (1995–2001). Looking out from Windsong over our swimming pool to the beautiful Pacific Ocean. I never tired of that view.

Patrón bottles—A sampling of the Patrón bottle evolution, beginning with one of the early glass stopper versions (second from left).

two assistants. It was nothing like a conventional brand headquarters. People who walked in were blown away and inspired by its beauty.

The main house was not a sprawling mansion typical of the area, but the scale of every room and the light at different times of day were magnificent. Of course the kitchen was a gourmet cook's delight; it was to become the warm and convivial center of our home. The house had an open floor plan with views everywhere you looked, perfect for entertaining. To the west, past the swimming pool, was a sweeping panorama of cliffs and sea. To the east, the back of our house faced mountains and soft, green rolling hills. Many a full moon night, we lay in bed watching its bright rays dance on the ocean's surface.

The moment we moved in, Martin and I set about doing what we loved most: design. As in all things, we worked together seamlessly, shaping our new home into a work of art, decorating in off white accented with natural colored fabrics and gorgeous exotic wood pieces Martin had sourced from an artisan's workshop in Mexico. People thought we spent a fortune, but we didn't. We knew where to find the best.

On the grounds, I kept a beehive, grew fruits and vegetables, and tended to the hundreds of cymbidium orchid plants that came with the property. No detail was too small to be overlooked. Every inch of our new home became the object of our loving and painstaking attention until Windsong became the perfect outward expression of the harmony and beauty of our life together. Anyone entering would immediately be affected by this special energy.

EARLY RETIREMENT

Everyone enjoys the feeling of having arrived, and so did we. By no means were we multimillionaires. We didn't have the wealth of many of our friends and neighbors. But we were beyond comfortable.

Money was no longer an issue, and we could indulge ourselves without breaking the bank. It was all we needed.

Still, old habits die hard. I was still being cautious. Soon after settling into our new home, I was sitting by the pool with Martin when he suddenly turned to me and asked: "Why are you still working in your insurance business?"

"For the money," I replied.

"We don't need it. Retire from that business so you can be available to Patrón full time."

I agreed happily, but there was something else. Marriage had never been important to either of us. We'd both been married and divorced long ago, and it was a case of been there, done that. But with all these changes I was beginning to feel a little unsettled. While we were on the subject, I decided to say something:

"Babe, it's not that I want to be married, but I would at least like to know that you would want to marry me."

"Ilana, what are you talking about?" he replied. "You *are* my life. There's never been anyone else. We are one!"

"Yes, I know, but we've bought this house, and now I'm closing my business. We should form something secure."

"What would make you feel secure?" he asked.

"Well, nothing has my name on it."

"Nothing has my name on it either; it's all owned by corporations. Everything we are and everything we have is joined together; even marriage couldn't make it any closer," he said.

In my mind, it was enough.

MRS. PATRÓN

I began living and breathing the business full-time. As far as I was concerned, we were now Mr. and Mrs. Patrón. It was what Martin wanted, and I was thrilled to be living and fulfilling his dream, which had become mine too. What started as a fun adventure was growing into the most successful ultrapremium tequila company in the world, and I was eager to see it all the way through. My clients would be taken care of. Len, my brother-in-law, had recently qualified as a financial consultant, so I handed them over to him. That freed me to focus on many details of the business that Martin had less time for as sales of Patrón began to explode.

I promoted the brand whenever I could, wherever I happened to be. In the Patrón way, we set about introducing ourselves to the bar and restaurant owners of Montecito and the greater Santa Barbara area. We hosted tasting events all over that part of the California coast and made sure Patrón was available on every shelf, just as we had done in Los Angeles. It was a matter of expanding our personal footprint.

By then we had already gained considerable traction in most high-end establishments; therefore, we didn't need to educate everyone from scratch. Patrón's superb quality was already well understood by those in the know. But we made our presence felt in as many fabulous ways as possible, from trips to the local supermarkets, where merchandisers, shoppers, and stock boys greeted Martin like a celebrity and asked him to sign bottles, to visits to the most exclusive restaurants where celebrities and socialites dined. We were determined to be associated with a good time no matter where Patrón was consumed or sold.

Martin gifted me with riding lessons, so I got involved with the local horse crowd, befriending my riding instructor, the Norwegian beauty Nina Svele. Martin had owned Arabian racehorses at one time, and anything to do with horses was a passion of his as well. Thus, it was only natural to get involved as the main corporate sponsor when the world polo championships came to Santa Barbara in

1999. Like the yacht race, it was another chance to get Patrón branding out in front of national and international media, so we brought in six different Patrón Girls to work the event over the two weeks, setting up a VIP Patrón tent for the players and guests alike, serving them Patrón in all its variations. Of course, Nina was the perfect ambassador, because she was an excellent horsewoman who knew the scene. She had a ball in the VIP tent. When Brazil won in the final match against Argentina, there was a lot of celebrating to be done among those hot young Latin men all decked out in their mud-splattered riding chaps. Nina served them shots of iced Patrón, and they returned the favor by spraying her with Veuve Cliquot and tossing her up in the air. Not that she was complaining. I suspect she got a few dates out of that enviable situation.

Fun and glamour became our trademarks, but our Patrón lifestyle could be about something as simple as entertaining at home, yet another favorite activity of ours. We would regularly host either a dinner where Martin would dazzle guests with his gourmet meals and Patrón-laced concoctions or a blowout party that people would talk about for years afterward. Our kitchen was our laboratory, where Martin was both chef and mixologist (long before mixology was even a term in bartending), plying guests with creations such as the Patrón margarita.

Unlike the traditional margarita, it was not made with lime but with a grapefruit soda called Squirt and a shot of Patrón and Citronge. The bubbles from the Squirt had the added benefit of making it seem as though the alcohol reached the bloodstream more quickly for an immediate Patrón high.

The idea of mixing a margarita with lime was actually a bastardization of the traditional Mexican recipe using *limones*, which are much less tart than regular limes or lemons. Since we couldn't get *limones* in the United States, we came up with this alternative. Martin's version was much less harsh and citrusy than the gut-burning lime juice versions usually served in bars to better complement the clean taste of Patrón Silver. It was genius, because the whole idea of bar sales was to get people to drink as much as possible. The smoother the drink, the more people consume. While it wasn't always possible to obtain Squirt, many bars followed our lead and developed a softer, sweeter variation of the Patrón margarita.

THE LABORATORY

Martin used Patrón and Citronge in the kitchen the way the Italians use olive oil. He believed there were healthful properties. Together, we created fabulous desserts such as Patrón-laced sorbets, cookies, and a key lime pie. It was used in salsas and ceviche, perfectly complemented with ingredients such as cilantro, lime, and homegrown avocado. A few months after we moved in, we had the perfect excuse to introduce ourselves, our creativity, and our brand with a huge party for Martin's birthday. It wasn't going to be a surprise party, because I'd had that done to me before and it had been a very strange, disjointed experience. Not that it was ever easy to surprise Martin. Besides, he was using one of the guesthouses as his office while the greenhouse was undergoing reconstruction, so I had to tell him as guests would be flying in to celebrate.

"Martin, when do you expect to be finished?" I asked him.

"I don't know, babe; soon. Why?"

"Well, you might want to have it ready in time for your birthday, because I've got guests arriving who will need to sleep in your temporary office. And I'm sure you'd love to show off your new headquarters."

That got him. Martin was nothing if not house-proud, so the offices were completed just in time. About 80 people from all over the world would be there to celebrate. But Martin had no idea what else was in store for him. While he was out, I had a wall draped in black fabric festooned with ribbons in Patrón green. I had little black cards made with holes punched in each corner, where guests could write a rhyme about Martin in white pencil, which we then tied onto the fabric. There was a stand where partiers could enjoy freshly shucked oysters. I hired a top Japanese chef and set up a sushi bar where he prepared fresh sashimi and rolls. In the dining room I'd constructed a table draped in fabric and laden with desserts from an eminent pastry chef. But the real treat was yet to come.

In our first few months at Windsong we'd acquainted ourselves with an establishment called the Spearmint Rhino in Santa Barbara. It was the local strip club. One of the women who worked there, Erin, was so gorgeous and elegant that we decided to hire her as a Patrón Girl. I went down to the club to hire some dancers as additional eye candy for Martin's party, with Erin as the feature attraction.

As the sun set and steam rose from the heated pool, guests began to see the topless girls dancing in the distance, their figures silhouetted through the moonlit mist like the Three Graces. On the other side of the house, French doors opened the living room to a courtyard where the previous owner had kept parrots. He'd left behind a stunning giant parrot cage built of white walls and curved bars, which was where the girls ultimately ended up. They were exotic creatures of a different sort. Our gorgeous go-go girls were creating a buzz as Martin's favorite music played.

Meanwhile, I had snuck Erin into the dining room and under the pastry table, where we'd created a fake birthday cake as the centerpiece. Our contractor had cut a hole in the center of the table and attached handles underneath it. We lit the candles, and I gathered everyone around to sing "Happy Birthday." Martin blew out the candles, and all of a sudden the fake cake lifted up and a naked Erin emerged, wearing nothing but thigh-high black stiletto boots. She stepped out, picked one of the strawberries from a dessert, dipped it in melted chocolate, and seductively licked it off before redipping it and feeding it to Martin. Earlier, I'd set up three trays behind the cake with red, white, and blue paint, each with its own miniroller. As a sexy song played, Erin began the dance I'd choreographed for her the day before, sashaying by the trays and painting her left boob blue. A few moments later, she went back to the tray and painted three red stripes across her torso and one on her right breast. Finally, toward the end of the song, she returned to paint white stripes between the red with a few spots on her left boob. Martin and our guests went wild seeing the American flag, at which point I threw her a large white T-shirt, which she laid out on the ground and imprinted with her patriotically painted body. Then Erin handed the self-stamped flag T-shirt to the birthday boy, which he absolutely loved.

The rest of the naked girls made their way inside and started dancing with the guests. My nephews, who by then were in their late teens, got quite an eyeful. By the end of the evening, the girls were offering lap dances and a few of the wives and girlfriends were doing sexy little dances for their husbands. Although it was fairly innocent and by no means an orgy, a few people left in disgust. That was our introduction to Santa Barbara society.

Admittedly, we got a little carried away at times. Warwick loves to remind me about the time the four of us went to dinner at the San Ysidro Ranch, one of the finest hotels in North America. By the time Warwick and his wife arrived at our house to pick us up, Martin and I had already enjoyed a couple of Patrón cocktails. We were a giggling mess, and Warwick was highly amused.

When we arrived at the restaurant, we must have made an impression, because we were taken straight through the dining room and seated out on the veranda. We could not have looked more out of place. Martin was his usual unapologetic self, with his long dark hair, black shirt, black tuxedo jacket, and cowboy boots, like an aging rock star, whereas I looked like his bohemian chic blonde groupie. The rest of the diners looked like typical denizens of conservative Santa Barbara; the women wore Lily Pulitzer dresses, and their men's uniforms consisted of checked button-down shirts, blue blazers, and khakis. Perhaps the maitre d' felt it was safer to seat us outside, away from the rest, and that was probably just as well as Martin and Warwick puffed away on cigars. I'm not sure if it was generally allowed, but no one was about to stop us, as we were ordering everything on the menu, including expensive vintage wines.

At one point, Martin turned around and saw many of the other diners inside staring at our group, open-mouthed. The fact that we were providing the entertainment struck us as so funny that we burst into peals of helpless laughter. It was typical of the high life we led back then.

SERIOUS BUSINESS

But contrary to appearances, we were all business 90 percent of the time, and even when we were entertaining ourselves and others, it served a purpose.

What began in blissful ignorance as a fun adventure became a serious business that was growing exponentially every year, and we had to get much more savvy and sophisticated in the way we managed the brand. We realized that we had the potential to become huge, but when you are dealing in consumable products and trying to get to the next level, it's necessary to spend and spend big. Of course, Martin wasn't doing this just for fun. But you cannot chase the dollar. Even at that highly developmental stage, nothing was ever done just for the money. We had to keep stuffing the pipeline, investing in the business without obsessing about how much we were going to sell that day. It was about maintaining that fine balance between having fun and remaining focused on the details of the present moment.

As long as you are structured and have somewhat of a plan, the monthly bills don't come as a surprise. We always knew when and how much we would have to pay for the packaging, the utilities, payroll, shipping, and the like. We were managing our finances in such a way that we were easily able to cover our monthly nut and then some. Running our business didn't cost much in comparison to our competitors. We'd gotten a good deal on our own warehouse, an asset that eliminated costs for storage and housed the offices as well. There weren't many mouths to feed. Each time we moved to a better distribution company, we received more marketing dollars, giving us yet more cash to spend on building the brand and expanding our capacity and giving us enough to deal with the unforeseen problems that continued to plague production.

DROUGHT AND DISEASE

It's just as well we'd accrued a financial cushion, because potentially catastrophic problems still occurred. In 1997, a severe shortage of agave threw the tequila business into crisis. About a third of the agave harvest had been devastated by disease and environmental damage, according to reports at the time.[1] Many farmers, meanwhile, had been planting alternative crops, creating a severe shortage of the raw material just as this liquor category was on the verge of a boom. Added to this unfortunate circumstance was a human-made disaster: Jose Cuervo.

Because pure agave tequila is expensive and difficult to produce, some manufacturers cut it with other substances, such as grain alcohol. Cuervo, the world's largest producer of tequila, was suspected of being one of the worst culprits of this. But a product cannot legally be called tequila unless at least 51 percent of its sugars come from agave, so the tequila giant was under suspicion. While it was never proven, the Tequila Regulatory Council of Mexico calculated that based on the amount of agave Cuervo was buying, they could not have the minimum amount of agave in their tequila. It's my understanding that the tequila board gave Cuervo six months to either bring the agave content up to the required percentage or remove the word *tequila* from the product. In response, Cuervo, a huge business with deep pockets, became a major agave investor, buying up all the agave it could. I would only be speculating to suggest this move was intended to cover their tracks and make it impossible to calculate how much agave they were actually using, but it had the net effect of locking up most of the available agave on the market.

It put the entire industry up the creek. It was so bad that agave thefts became commonplace and Cuervo reportedly had to hire more than 100 security guards to protect the precious commodity growing in its fields. The plants had become so rare, they earned the nickname "blue gold." No one could get agave, and many of the smaller, boutique brands died off.

It was a perfect storm for the tequila industry: fewer and fewer fields dedicated to growing agave as a result of blight and frost and a corporation hoarding what was left. It messed up the market for a long time, because it takes years for the *pinas* to develop to the right size and the sugar levels have to be exactly right. The supply problem was not one that could be corrected overnight, so some desperate tequila producers were even harvesting plants at five and six years, when the sugar content was nowhere near what it should be.

But in many ways this disaster was good for us. One of the family owners of our factory was married to the ex-mayor of the town with the best Blue Weber agave fields in the region, and he happened to own fields. He had to be one of the few farmers in Mexico who wasn't selling to Cuervo, so we had our own exclusive supplier.

Some things will always remain out of your control, but there is plenty you can do to insulate your business against negative external forces, whether that means shoring up your suppliers through strong relationships or building enough of a financial cushion to weather the storm. Luckily, we had done both.

STILL STANDING

Of course, we had to pay a premium for our agave supply. Between 1997 and 2000, the price had tripled. But it was well worth the extra investment, because the agave shortage had effectively expanded our market share. Over the months, we could literally see boutique brands of tequila appear and disappear. Very few of the upstarts were able to stick. We were surviving and thriving because we were among the very few producers of ultrapremium tequila who could persevere. The fact that Patrón was able to consistently maintain its high standards for quality throughout the shortage not only solidified our base of loyal customers but enhanced our reputation in new markets around the country.

One especially smart decision Martin made around this time was to introduce Patrón Reposado, which was aged six months in French white oak barrels, versus the one year it took to produce Patrón Anejo. Eventually, the Silver did outpace the sales of our aged Patrón— a first in the history of the tequila business. But in the first few years, the ratio of Silver and Gold sales was about the same. People used to prefer the aged tequila because it smoothed out some of the rough edges, although that wasn't an issue with Patrón Silver, which was already perfectly smooth. It was more a matter of personal preference.

I happen to like the cleaner taste of the Silver best, but many enjoy the amber tint and smokier oak flavor of the aged tequila. Reposado gave our customers another option. When your brand is hot, it never hurts to expand your line of products, and the shorter production time compared with the Anejo or Gold meant we would have more tequilas available in the market at a faster pace. It could only be to our advantage during the agave crisis.

BRANCHING OUT

Meanwhile, we had entered a honeymoon phase with Seagram's. With the cushion of their considerable resources behind us and the extra revenue we were generating with our now extensive sales force, Martin decided it was also time to expand the business in other ways. It was his dream to develop a premium line of the top-selling spirit categories, applying what we'd learned by redefining the tequila market to these new products. It made perfect sense to start with a premium sipping rum, the second highest selling spirit next to vodka and a tired category that was poised for growth.[2] It too was from the Caribbean, distilled from indigenous crops and made popular by the colonizers and traders of the New World. Rum was also something that was usually consumed with mixers, but Martin was determined to change that by blending some of the finest aged rums from all over the West Indies.

Developing the new product involved some island hopping. Martin loved the Caribbean and we were particularly fond of exploring the cultures, so it was a thrill for us to go on another adventure, seeking out small rum factories from Venezuela to Guyana. It was also an excuse to build another base in Anguilla, a place we loved to call our second home. Since we knew we'd be spending a lot more time there, we bought a place on the beach. Martin set up an aging, blending, and bottling facility on the island of Anguilla and flew Francisco in many times to help him and oversee the entire process. The new rum plant created the first "industry" for Anguilla without any waste or pollution. Until then, tourism was all that Anguilla lived off, so the local government loved us.

That's how Pyrat Rum was born. The product was smooth and rich, using the best the islands had to offer. Again, Martin chose the name and liked the old spelling of *pirate* to evoke the era when rum first came into being. He designed the squat, rounded, and corked decanter to resemble the vessels used by rum runners and ship captains in the 1800s. Like Patrón bottles, each was handblown and numbered, and they quickly became collector's items as well. I added a sunset orange ribbon around its neck in a more swashbuckling fashion than the Patrón ribbon and a little metal *hotei* charm. Martin and I had found and bought a beautiful wooden sculptured *hotei* about 30 inches tall whose image became the one on the bottle. *Hotei* is one of seven Japanese lucky gods who, among other things, is the patron saint of restaurants and bartenders.

SOUS CHEF

We were getting bigger by the month, but only in terms of sales. Unlike the rest of the spirits industry, in which each category had long been dominated by the big corporate brands—Cuervo, Bacardi, Jack Daniels, Smirnoff—we remained resolutely small and entrepreneurial, growing at our own steadfast pace. Part of our success was that we did not get acquired or, rather, gobbled up by one of the liquor giants, as many other new boutique brands did the moment they showed any signs of success.

We held on to our independence as hundreds of imitators started up and quickly fell by the wayside. This allowed us to be nimble and react quickly to the many and varied challenges of the market-place. More important, it allowed us to stay true to our brand's message. As Ted Simpkins, our dear friend at Southern Wine & Spirits (who is now at Young's Market Company), once told me, the problem with the large liquor companies is that they tend to change the head of marketing every two years. This person has no history with the brand and wants to make his or her mark by scrapping the old marketing campaign and creating something completely new. There is no consistency of message, and the customer gets confused.

At Patrón it was just us. Martin remained in full control. Of course, when you are small and growing exponentially, there are also challenges. If cloning had been an option, we might have gone for it. New locations, new products, and an expanding footprint for sales meant Martin and I were constantly traveling, and we still had only a few people on staff. It fell to me to look after some of the additional operational details. The way I viewed it, I was Martin's sous chef. He was in charge, but if something needed to be chopped, peeled, or blanched, it was my pleasure to do so. At one point I was managing the finances, creating operating systems, overseeing payroll, hiring and training office staff, and answering the numerous e-mails and letters from Patrón customers and fans.

I was actively included in all the decisions. We lived and breathed the business morning, noon, and night, to the point where we occasionally had to remind ourselves to talk about other things. Yet we were having so much fun with Patrón and each other despite the many challenges we faced. There was no competition between us.

Martin was extremely proud of my contributions, to the point where he would boast to all our dinner guests about every little thing I did, whether it was a particularly artful invitation, a flower arrangement, or the dessert I'd made that night. I didn't even have to be within earshot. If I happened to be in the other room, my dear friend Nina would often report back to me about something my biggest cheer-leader would say to the assembled crowd. He was like a proud papa. That was one of the many reasons why she loved him.

Most couples don't live their lives quite so symbiotically and maybe it was not the healthiest thing ultimately, but for us it worked. Our private life, the business, the finances, everything, blended to-gether seamlessly. As Martin said, we were all one, and there were no boundaries between the different aspects of our lives. We had no set roles. We didn't live and work in separate corners.

Concocting marketing and promotional events and designing ads, packaging, and giveaways gave me the greatest pleasure of all because those activities allowed me to unleash my creative side, and there were no limits. The parties gave us the opportunity to make our customers and sales representatives feel valued and appreciated. Too many of the competing products our teams had to sell came from large corporations that lacked the personal touch, so inviting and entertaining them in style was a key way to stand out against all the other spirits fighting for space on liquor store shelves.

One of my favorite among those projects was the 1999 launch party for our first major paid advertising campaign, "Taste the Magic," in the Barker Hangar at the Santa Monica Airport. I had a 35,000-square-foot space to work with, and it was a daunting task that took months of planning. We were expecting more than 700 re-tailers and sales reps from across California, and I wanted them to associate our brand with class, beauty, and fun from the moment they walked into the space. Patrón's distinctive green, black, and silver colors festooned the entire space, from the tables to the rafters. Each table had a centerpiece of lush white tuberoses held by empty Patrón bottles, and their heavenly perfume filled the air.

A fitting detail of the invitation-only event was to be a competition for the most creatively decorated Patrón bottle. All 25 of the entries were on display, and they wouldn't have been out of place in an art gallery. Guests produced beautifully hand-painted and -decorated empties, a fish tank, and, the winning design, a whimsical Patrón lamp. The winner got an all-expenses-paid trip to a five-star resort in Cabo, Mexico.

For the grand finale, we'd arranged for a spectacular magic trick to be performed by our charming magician friend, Simon. The challenge was to create a trick that would be large-scale enough to captivate everyone in the room, a seemingly impossible task, but somehow he'd managed it. As the guests were buzzing with excitement over this feast of the senses, Karen McDougal, *Playboy* magazine's 1998 Playmate of the Year and our favorite Patrón Girl, took the stage. The dark-haired beauty, featured in our print ads, was to be part of the magic act. With much fanfare, Simon put her in a chest and made her disappear. A split second later, you could hear a collective gasp from the audience as Karen appeared up in the rafters on the opposite side of the hangar.

The whole event was designed to celebrate a billboard and print ad campaign featuring Karen. For the front of the ad, I styled Karen in a white tuxedo pantsuit with a white top hat and a Patrón green silk bowtie and kerchief peeking out of the breast pocket of her matching white waistcoat, which perfectly set off her long chocolate brown hair. She had a gorgeous body, with curves in all the right places, but the ad was exactly the right balance between sexy and chic. In the picture, Karen held out her left hand, which had a Patrón Silver bottle levitating above it. Underneath was our tagline: "Taste the Magic."

The big surprise came when you turned the page and saw the twin ad for Patrón XO. We hired Joanne Gair, the brilliant body painter best known for her work on Demi Moore's infamous 1992 *Vanity Fair* cover, where she'd painted a delightfully cheeky *trompe l'oeil* birthday suit on the actress. On the reverse side of our ad, we did the same thing, but in the Patrón XO colors. A rear shot showed a nude Karen standing in the same position as she was in the front of the ad, except that we were looking at her from behind, "wearing" painted white tuxedo pants and suspenders, with a purple kerchief sticking out of her "back pocket." She was holding up a levitating bottle of Patrón XO. Underneath was the tagline "More Magic."

It took Joanne eight hours to paint that bodysuit, but she did such a fantastic job for us that we hired her again many times, and we became good friends. The ad also started a trend of using Playboy Playmates in the advertising for all our product lines. The implication was clear: "Taste the magic; be a part of this lifestyle that is associated with beautiful Playboy Playmates." It was Martin's idea, and it certainly got us a lot of attention. In fact, I believe this is how Hugh Hefner came upon the idea of having "painted ladies" serve drinks at all his parties at the Playboy Mansion.

Our "Taste the Magic" launch was just one of numerous events I'd organized to promote Patrón, and it was such a privilege to have the opportunity to indulge my blossoming creativity. I've always prided myself on being able to throw one hell of a party. But it was a great joy to be able to use my skills and experience across all aspects of the business. At this point, I was overseeing a complicated financial structure. With factories, warehousing, offices, and bank accounts all over the world, money was moving around the globe in large sums. While Martin kept a tight grip on the money movement, he didn't have the accounting skills and meticulous eye for detail that was necessary to enforce strict financial security systems and cover all the bases.

But more than anything, I was Martin's companion. Building a business can be a lonely road, but the beauty of a true partnership is that someone always has your back. Never was that more necessary than when the marriage with Seagram's started to sour.

ON THE ROCKS

The foundation of that relationship was beginning to unravel. For Seagram's, the distribution deal had to include the option to buy 51 percent equity in Patrón after five years at the industry standard formula of 10 times the bottom line. When we were negotiating the deal, Martin was prepared to give them 49 percent, but they piled on the pressure to sign on their terms. Martin finally agreed because we were in separate negotiations to build a factory together. Martin felt that as long as he was in control of the supply from the factory, he would at least have some kind of leverage.

Seagram's did what it was supposed to do according to the contract and bought the minimums, but they could afford to shelve the bottles in their warehouse and sell as little as possible for five years, thereby controlling the ultimate value of the company when they could contractually buy in. The deal also provided that either party could opt out of the contract after three years without cause. It took Martin less than that amount of time to realize what they were up to, so he decided to bail in 1999, at the precise three-year mark of the distribution deal.

There was already bad blood between Martin and the liquor giant. As it built its new tequila factory, Seagram's wanted to go bigger and bigger. Against advice and urging from both Martin and Francisco, they built a distillery using huge steel vats instead of the small wooden containers used in the original factory, so that the tequila didn't ferment in the same way.

At the factory opening, Martin; JP; Seagram's chairman, Edgar Bronfman, Jr.; and I were all flown into Jalisco by helicopter to join high-ranking Mexican politicians for the "celebration." But you could have cut the tension with the giant scissors that were used to snip the ribbon and officially open the factory. During the party afterward, toasts and speeches were made. We toughed it out with frozen smiles, and Martin did his best to play the game and refrain from rolling his eyes. But the goodwill between Martin and Seagram's had already dwindled past the point of no return.

In his and Francisco's minds, they had committed the cardinal sin of compromising on quality. In their eagerness to create volume, Seagram's had overlooked the production details that give Patrón its unique flavor. Distilling in such large batches ruined the taste. Martin was made aware of the situation through regular reports from Francisco, who was beside himself with frustration. Martin continued to complain to the executives at Seagram's and became a thorn in their side. But he was absolutely right. The tequila did taste burnt. For this reason, it was never used for Patrón.

TASTE TEST PART II

The Seagram's executives did not agree, so to prove his point, Martin called for a blind taste test at JP's home in Malibu. Just as was done for the taste test at Spago, he enlisted professional food and wine critics to get the consensus. Everyone, including Seagram's executives, had to agree that not only did the batch produced in their factory not taste like Patrón, it was not even a good-tasting tequila.

"Martin, don't worry about it. People are buying the bottle and the name, not the liquid inside. They won't even know the difference," said one executive.

Martin was appalled and made it clear that he would not be buying their version of tequila for Patrón. There was no way in hell he was going to put his brand's name on it. For obvious reasons, both Martin and JP removed themselves from the factory deal long before it was built.

They would not break the cardinal rule: quality above all else. Never be distracted from the fundamental importance that everything that is great and differentiating about your product should be maintained and always exceed expectations. Remember, you are your own best customer, so follow your own high standards.

The factory departure was tolerated, but when Martin walked away from the distribution deal, all bets were off. He was justifiably furious at the way his brand was being held hostage in their warehouse, which was a direct result of his naiveté in not insisting on a minimum sell clause in the original contract. By then, Martin was determined to make them pay for any loss of business. But Seagram's launched a bitter counterattack and sued for breach of contract. The ensuing three-month trial without a jury became a classic David and Goliath battle, with Seagram's army of corporate lawyers and paid "experts" pitted against Martin. We were in over our heads.

I was terrified that the stress would wreak havoc with Martin's heart condition. We were staying in a hotel room in Los Angeles, living, breathing, eating, and dreaming the trial. It was a fight for the very survival of Patrón as we knew it, and I had no idea how we were going to make it through. Martin was in to win at all costs, and he fought the case with all he had. But we lost. Martin had gone into it expecting to be compensated, but instead the court ordered us to buy back all the stockpiled product, plus interest and costs, to the tune of around $28 million, as I recall. They eventually settled for several million less.

FALLOUT

JP stood by us throughout the trial, but it was only years later that I learned how much he had questioned Martin's wisdom in going to war.

"Ilana, Seagram's weren't trying to ruin us," JP told me recently. "We wanted to go our own way, and contractually we owed them money for that privilege."

During the trial, there was a protracted and detailed accounting of how much they paid us for inventory and the amount they were required to spend on marketing. For every container of tequila delivered and paid for by Seagram's, we had to kick back a set amount toward advertising and promotions, and it was Martin's contention that they had not spent these monies according to their contractual obligation, which was why he felt he was owed.[3] But JP wanted Martin to negotiate with Seagram's outside the courtroom. In his usual smooth fashion, he believed it would have been possible to make peace and call it even, but when we were approached by Seagram's, Martin's response was, "How much are they going to pay me?"

It was just one of many things that were creating tension between Martin and JP. JP, who once told Martin that he was the bank, would not cover the debt, nor would he cosign a bank loan, always insisting on his no-debt policy. Martin was stuck. I was disappointed but couldn't blame him. It is how JP has always conducted business and is a large part of why he has been so successful. He did, however, concede to Martin's desperate plea, officially allowing him to go out on his own and seek financing for the debt without his cosign.

JP may have had his doubts, but Martin still had my total support. Whether it involved sending out cease and desist orders to the start-up brands that were trying to copy our packaging or fighting to win back control of distribution from Seagram's, Martin was doing all he could to keep the integrity of the Patrón brand, and I never questioned it.

Ultimately, the heavy burden of the decision making landed on his shoulders. We were by no means equals in the business, and I was just fine with that. He was the driver, and I rode shotgun and helped him navigate our journey. Our roles were not so rigidly defined, and each one of us simply stepped in to do whatever was needed at the time. But Martin was very much in charge, although it was never said.

THE IRON CURTAIN

There was only one occasion when I wasn't 100 percent on board. It was getting to the point where I shuddered every time Martin came up with another idea, because it wasn't a matter of if it would happen but when. By the late 1990s we were traveling constantly between Los Angeles, Anguilla, and, in Martin's case, Mexico. We'd also recently opened an office and warehouse in Las Vegas. It was exhausting to be constantly on the move. And now Martin had the dream of buying a vodka factory in Poland, which would have effectively doubled the size of the business.

I had no idea how we were going to pull it off. The Seagram's trial had been draining him both physically and financially, and Martin still hadn't resolved the matter of how he was going to pay the money to Seagram's. I was concerned that he was overreaching, so I was less than enthusiastic when he announced we'd be going.

"Pack your bags, Ilana, we're going to Warsaw."

"Honey, do you really need me to come this time?"

"Yes, I need you there. We're meeting with the minister of the treasury. This is big."

"Okay, babe; I'll be ready."

Martin rarely took important meetings without me. He was severely lacking in diplomatic skills, and to his great credit, he knew it. People either loved him or hated him, and his bombastic style could suck the oxygen right out of the room. He almost always did what he said he was going to do no matter how impossibly ambitious it sounded, but people tended to dismiss what he was saying as mere bluster. It could even be about something as small as a meal. At one of the first dinner parties we hosted at our home for John Paul and Eloise, JP pulled me aside and asked, "Ilana, did Martin really cook all this himself?"

He was referring to the spectacular gourmet meal that we had just enjoyed.

"Yes, JP. Martin did it all himself, from scratch."

Similarly, the Polish factory owners wanted to know that Martin was a man who would execute. I was there for the very serious purpose of lending him credibility at high-level meetings with factory owners, trade officials, and heads of state. I had to demonstrate that what appeared to be all talk was actually possible by laying out the options and discussing the various ways a plan could be realistically executed. In that way, we balanced each other perfectly, and Martin always proudly introduced me as his partner in crime.

INTERNATIONAL DIPLOMACY

So off to Warsaw we went. The trip took place in the early summer of 2001 while the country was still playing economic catch-up after so many decades behind the Iron Curtain and many state-owned enterprises were having to privatize and adapt to free market forces. The country's transition from a centrally planned economy in the early 1990s had been rough, and any momentum gained by the late 1990s had been crushed by the Russian financial crisis in 1999 and then the global recession in 2001. This made state officials and business owners more than a little gun-shy about going into business with foreign investors.

The government had only recently decided to privatize the vodka industry, which it rightly considered a national treasure, yet it saw in other countries, such as the Czech Republic, cases of large liquor companies taking over indigenous beer and spirit companies and then closing factories left and right. The Polish leadership wanted to protect Polish interests, and we had to convince everyone that this would not be the kind of takeover that would involve downsizing. For this deal to go through, it was imperative that they trust us.

Vodka was and still is the number one selling spirit in the world, and top-shelf vodkas were becoming white hot in the liquor industry. It was Martin's dream to own not only a great brand but the factory that produced it so that he would have complete control over quality and production this time. I found out much later that JP wasn't entirely with him on this either. Although he eventually invested in his own brand, Ultimat Vodka, JP didn't want the headache of owning a vodka factory halfway around the world.

When we arrived, I sank into a gloom I just couldn't shake. The weather was dreary, and something about the place saddened me. I'm usually excited to land in a new place and explore the food and culture, but I barely had any desire to leave my hotel room. Perhaps it had something to do with the fact that my mother was a Polish Jew who'd been rounded up and sent to a camp during the Holocaust. Maybe the place was filled with the ghosts of my family members.

The most interesting part of the trip was the factory itself. The distillery, one of the oldest in the country, was Lancut, which controlled about 10 percent of the Polish vodka market. Situated just outside of Warsaw, it occupied a pristine eighteenth-century building that also housed a vodka museum. The factory happened to be built on a natural aquifer, which meant that the vodka was produced from the purest spring water. The biggest selling beverage in the world is water, so if nothing else, we could have bottled and sold this incredible-tasting H_2O. But forget about the water. The vodka was like nothing I'd ever tasted. There could be no doubt Martin would have had a unique, ultrapremium product to sell in this highly competitive spirit category. On paper, the deal would have made perfect sense if Martin had had more of a financial cushion and a supersonic jet to ferry him back and forth between continents.

Martin was prepared to offer the owners $7 million. I wasn't sure where he was going to get the money in light of what he still owed Seagram's. I found out only later that he'd mortgaged Windsong for the maximum he could get. The Polish dignitaries were hesitant. Like me, Martin had no intention of screwing anyone, but they didn't know what was in his heart. It was a question of convincing them that it had to work for everybody.

One night at dinner I was chitchatting with the government officers, who were asking me about Martin's history. I told them that when I first met him he'd been recovering from a bankruptcy. I described how he rose up from nothing, listing all that he'd achieved in his life completely on his own, without any special access or advantage. They were extremely impressed.

On our way back to the hotel, Martin quietly but sternly said: "I cannot believe you would disclose my bankruptcy to these people. Have you lost your mind?"

Whether it concerned his health or his finances, Martin didn't like people to know he was ever anything less than a successful alpha male, and he was pissed. But I felt that under the circumstances these people needed to know that he'd been through his own struggles and prevailed. He was furious with me, and that was a first for us.

"No, Martin, I haven't lost my mind. There's nothing wrong with it. It's fine. Own it. Look where you are today and all that you've achieved while always being scrupulously fair to the people you do business with."

It was not a harmonious trip. We weren't fighting per se, but neither of us had a skip in our step. When Martin had a meeting with the attorneys the next day to discuss the contract for the factory deal, I decided to stay in the hotel room and hide from the world. I had no desire to walk around and shop. Having booked a yacht in the Mediterranean, I spent time on my laptop planning our itinerary and hoping our next trip away could bring us closer somehow.

It was the first time in our relationship I felt like we were not perfectly in sync. I suppose one could say we were coming off our 12-year relationship high. Not that I was prepared to admit it. I wouldn't have walked away in a million years.

KINGS AND GODS

In the end, Martin bought the factory at the exact price he wanted to pay. His luck was turning, and after many months of rejections, it looked like he was about to get a break on a bank loan to pay back Seagram's as well. Revenues were as high as they had ever been in the history of the business, and Bacardi was sniffing around looking to buy the Patrón Tequila portion of the business for a low nine-figure sum. All of Martin's dreams were finally becoming a reality. He had gone way beyond his original goal of making back the money he'd lost in bankruptcy. Now he was a tequila mogul worth millions more.

But the bigger we became, the less victorious it felt in the whole scheme of things. My world, which was Martin, had changed. I still wasn't willing to acknowledge it, but the curtain lifted briefly one night when we'd had our dear friend Gregg Gann over for dinner. As usual, we went out by the pool to enjoy the clear night air, a cigar, and a Patrón nightcap. That was when it got weird.

Martin seemed aloof, detached, and condescending, a complete contrast to the man I knew and loved. I don't know if success had gone to his head, if it was his health, or both. By then, his heart was slipping out of rhythm frequently regardless of his habits. Blood and oxygen weren't flowing through his body as they should, and it was causing both physical and mental strain, leading to some odd behavior. He told Gregg that the magic of Patrón had helped him rise above mortal life and that he was living out some sort of manifest destiny. Then he leaned back in his lounge chair, spread out his arms, looked up at the starry sky, and said: "I am like kings and gods. I should be able to have anything I want."

I'm not sure what was going on in Martin's mind when he made that statement, and it may well have been some throwaway remark he never intended to be taken seriously. But it made a poor impression. Appalled, Gregg made his excuses and left. He never came to visit us in Montecito again. Shortly afterward, in August 2001, the same week Martin was finally able to secure a loan to pay back the Seagram's debt, we broke up. Apparently, I was no longer one of the wants of this self-proclaimed king or god. Suddenly, my personal journey with Patrón was over.

PART III

SUSTAINABLE DEVELOPMENT

CHAPTER 7

A Rude Awakening

I T WAS A PERFECT, sunny California day, but a maelstrom was brewing, and I had no idea from which direction or when it would land.

I was on my way to sign a retainer agreement with my new lawyer, Barry Cappello, when I saw him. A stranger was at my gate, changing the code on the keypad. The sight of the intruder threw me into a flat panic, so I called Barry: "Someone's messing with the keypad to the front gate. What should I do?"

"Tell him to stop, leave immediately, or you will call the sheriff and have him arrested. He's trespassing. And Ilana, do not leave the property. We can take care of our business via fax."

I pulled up in the jeep, opened the door, and screamed, "What do you think you're doing? Get off my property! Leave now or I'm calling the cops! You've got no right!"

The uninvited locksmith was stunned. He must have thought I was a raving lunatic. He left without an argument, before he had a chance to finish the job.

From that moment I was housebound. I had to listen to Barry's advice. I couldn't take the chance of leaving the property and never being able to get back in but hated the idea of being trapped and isolated. I'd never felt more vulnerable. Or desperate.

Something had been bubbling ever since Martin had left on his Italian cruise two weeks earlier. At first, I was oblivious, but now my radar was up. I called my sister Sharon in Los Angeles. She knew me best, and even though I insisted that everything was okay, she could hear the strain in my voice. Len, her husband, was on the line as well.

"We're not comfortable with you being home alone at a time like this," Len said. "I'm driving up to Santa Barbara this afternoon to be with you."

"Are you out of your mind?" I replied. "It's Friday! With the traffic today it will take you three hours to get here. I'll be fine."

"It's not up for discussion," Len said. "Who knows what's going on or what the hell could happen. I'm coming."

Four hours later, I buzzed him in, relieved to see him. Before we kissed and hugged hello, he asked me in disbelief, "They destroyed the mailbox too?" Right then, it occurred to me to collect the mail as I was expecting an important package that day. Sure enough, the locksmith had left our mailbox wide open, and there was a gaping hole where a heavy-duty lock had been. It was a communal box that we shared with three of our neighbors, just a few yards down the street from our property gate, so with Len safely in the house I felt more comfortable going out to check.

Driving down our long, steep, winding driveway for the second time that day, en route to the mailbox, I encountered another stranger, this time in a black SUV parked just inside the gate. How had he gotten in? Who the hell was he? What was he doing there? I wondered.

I didn't recognize the car but knew this wasn't good. Windsong was in a countrified neighborhood that consisted of sprawling verdant hillside estates and private roads. People didn't come up here unless they were delivering something or were invited. I didn't know if he had slipped in unnoticed when Len arrived or if someone had given him the entry code. Either way, he was there, waiting, because his engine was turned off. Whatever he was doing on our property, he wasn't looking for directions.

It seemed Len had indeed arrived in the nick of time. I was too terrified to confront the intruder. My mind was spinning, trying to make sense of all this. Instead, I drove right past him, through the open gate, across East Valley Road, and up our neighbor's service road behind some bushes. This afforded me a view of our entrance. Fearful and curious, I wanted to see what was happening. My heart was pounding out of my chest. I called Len, shrieking hysterically: "Len, Len! There's *another* strange man on our property. He's inside, *inside* the gate! What do we do?"

"Calm down and get back up here as soon as you can. But be careful!"

"Lock all the doors and windows!" I told him.

As we hung up, from my perch I witnessed a blue sedan pull up to the gate, punch in a code, and drive in. The two vehicles disappeared into the lush foliage as they wound their way up our drive. I freaked out. Len was here to save my arse, and now two strange men were heading his way.

I couldn't fathom what could happen; if Len was harmed, I'd never forgive myself. I was no longer thinking, just reacting in abject terror. Desperate to get back to the house to protect him somehow, I put the car in gear and gunned it back across the street. Just as I clicked open our gate, the two cars reappeared after looping around the circle at the top of the drive and were heading back down the hill. By this time I was more hysterical, shaking and livid. I rolled down my window and screamed like a madwoman: "Get off my property. *Get off my property!* You're trespassing! I'm calling the police!"

"We're sorry. We made a mistake; we weren't meant to be here. If you get out of our way, we'll leave," they said, pulling out of the gate and up onto my neighbor's drive, where I'd just been.

I drove inside, the gate closed, and I wrenched my jeep into park. Throwing open the door, I stood up on the sideboard, nervously observing over the top of the jeep as the two strapping young men got out of their cars and just stood there, talking to each other. It was clear they weren't going anywhere.

Suddenly, brakes were screeching and several cars were skidding into a semicircle right outside, blocking East Valley Road in each direction. It looked like a scene from *Mod Squad*. The county sheriff and his backup team got out of their cars and paused. Just at that moment, a white BMW sedan emerged into the middle of the circle and Martin stepped out of the car. That was when it occurred to me: Holy shit, they're here for me! What have I done?

All I wanted to do was escape and get back to the house, but by now Len had come looking for me, and his car was blocking mine and facing the wrong way. There was no other choice but for him to reverse up the hill. I parked my jeep across the drive so that the other cars couldn't pass, locked the doors, and flew into Len's passenger seat. He couldn't go fast enough for me.

"Go, *go, goooo!* Faster, Len, *faster!*" I screamed like a woman deranged. It felt like we were running for our lives. Our property stretched over seven acres, and it was a long walk up the hill, so that would buy us some time before they reached the house.

When we got there, I immediately called Barry to describe the mayhem.

"I don't know why they're there, but whatever it is, do what they tell you," Barry said. "But move as slowly as humanly possible," he added.

Soon afterward, Martin and his entourage stormed into the

kitchen. Everyone followed suit, and the room filled up with at least a dozen men. The sheriff stepped forward and presented me with some papers—the ultimate blow: "Ms. Edelstein? I have a kick-out order. I need to remove you from the premises immediately. Mr. Crowley has been kind enough to pay for a room at the San Ysidro Ranch for you, so go and pack a few things for the night."

In my entire life I'd never done anything illegal or even remotely unethical. There'd been no run-ins with the law besides a couple of traffic infractions. I'd always been a law-abiding citizen who paid her taxes and went out of her way to do the right thing. Yet here was the county sheriff attempting to escort me out of my home like some sort of miscreant. The shock to my very being was so immense that it felt physical, as if my head were struck between two crashing cymbals.

The court had been told that I was a dangerous and violent meth addict. All five feet three inches of me was clearly a physical threat, and I was not to be trusted in the house alone.

Worse, the love of my life had now become "Mr. Crowley." The fact that he was putting me up in a fancy hotel did nothing to lessen the sting. How could thousand-thread-count sheets bring comfort while my heart was breaking into a million little pieces? It was to be the same place where we had spent that hilarious evening with our dear friend Warwick Miller and the scene of some of my fondest memories, just one of many painful reminders of what we'd lost.

Inside, I was dying. I'd never felt more consumed with dread. Surrounded by armed men, stripped of my dignity, I wanted to throw up. The room started spinning, my knees buckled, and I collapsed into a sobbing heap on the floor. The middle of the kitchen, the center of our hearth and home and the focal point of so much love, warmth, and laughter during our years together, at once became the nexus of my lightest and darkest hours.

THE END OF THE AFFAIR

It wasn't supposed to end that way.

Our 13-year love affair had run its course. Together we'd lived a fabulous life of parties, adventure, spontaneity, and romance. Together we'd created and nurtured Patrón Tequila and enjoyed all the extravagance, indulgence, and beauty that go with it. But it wasn't just about that. What Martin and I had shared was real, and I'd never felt more valued, respected, and adored.

He was the first man to ever make me feel like I could do anything. If I came up with an idea for decorating our office or branding a new line of Patrón, he'd execute it and later boast about my accomplishments to anyone who would listen. Once, when we were browsing together at an antique store in the Sonoma Valley, my eyes lit upon a vintage top hat that belonged to the owner, and he steadfastly refused to sell it. But Martin somehow procured it, because on Valentine's Day weeks later, long after I'd forgotten about it, it appeared on my pillow. He lived to surprise and delight me and always did. Over the course of our relationship, he never stopped showering me with affection. No matter how he was with other people, we shared everything and lived our life together in nearly perfect harmony. That feeling didn't change just because the spark between us had burned out.

Two months earlier, Martin had ended things over dinner in the middle of a crowded restaurant, also at San Ysidro Ranch. Crushed, I went straight home and couldn't get out of bed for two days. But weeks later I actually thanked Martin for ending things when he did. I'd have clung to what we had even without the magic, and that would not have been good for either of us. Instead, we were doing things nicely. When couples around us split up, neither of us understood the point of all that acrimony. We'd always said that if two civilized adults could get into a relationship, they surely could get out of it with kindness and compassion.

Not that it was a clean break. When you share that much of your life together, it never is. In everything, from the business to our day-to-day lives at home, we were totally intertwined, and that kind of union takes a while to gently unravel. Two months after our breakup, we were still living together at Windsong. When I suggested finding myself somewhere else to rent and live until my new house was out of escrow, Martin objected and insisted that I move into one of our two guesthouses. When I did, he moved right in with me. The next day, we went back to living in the main house together.

We couldn't bear to be apart. It was ridiculous. We were still sleeping together, still having great sex. That side of our lives hadn't changed. Even though we were no longer in love, we'd always love each other. There'd always be some sort of togetherness. You can't just turn off the tenderness like a spigot. Or so I thought.

Several weeks before our breakup, Martin had chartered a luxury yacht in the Mediterranean. The plan was for the two of us to cruise around for a week in the Italian islands and just enjoy ourselves and each other. We traveled a lot for Patrón, but we hadn't had a proper vacation in five years. When Martin announced over our breakup dinner that he was going anyway, I understood. He converted it into a marketing opportunity for Patrón, inviting E! Entertainment's Brooke Burke and the producers of *Wild on E!* on board to shoot an episode featuring Patrón, starring himself, some friends of the brand, and a few Playboy bunnies. I couldn't go because our lives needed to take their separate courses.

I was depressed about missing this trip but also excited for Martin and the opportunity to get Patrón on television again, even packing the ladies' Patrón costumes and product swag for the journey. It gave me comfort to still play a small role, handling the back office logistics and continuing to manage some of the day-to-day operations from our home office. That freed Martin to do something positive and high-profile for the brand without the nagging worries of what might be happening during his absence.

Martin needed the break. Resolving the debt resulting from the trial took a toll on him. He was absolutely correct to challenge Seagram's for keeping our brand off the shelves in a thinly disguised effort to shrink our revenues. In business, you *are* your reputation. If you don't stand up for yourself, the Goliaths of this world will walk all over you.

In addition to recovering from the financial toll of the trial, Martin had been busy courting interest from Bacardi to buy the business. It was time to get serious and corporatize the business, so he hired Patrón's first chief financial officer to handle the paperwork and make it official. As a business, we were finally growing up.

But it was bittersweet. We'd sailed through the storm but could no longer enjoy the calm waters together. Of course we were still best friends. We would always be Mr. and Mrs. Patrón, just not in the romantic sense. It was time for each of us to move on, and so I thanked him for ending things when he did despite the pain I was feeling. Patrón had reached the heights of success, but unfortunately for us, it now became the only thing we had in common. We were no longer one, and I was numb. I should have known sooner, but truthfully, it would have never occurred to me to leave Martin. I would have gone on in that state forever.

UNWRITTEN PROMISES

Martin spent a week in London on business before heading to the Mediterranean. As always, we spoke at least once a day, sometimes twice. Our last few conversations had included how we were going to separate. We were figuring out ways I could live, since I'd long since given up my business and devoted all my energy to Patrón and supporting Martin's dream. At one stage, Martin offered me $10,000 a month for 10 years, plus household expenses, and instead of dividing up our furniture and belongings, he would pay for new furnishings. All I wanted was a firm commitment from him about how we would handle our affairs. It was time.

Martin was eager to assure me that he was as good as his word. I believed him, but a verbal agreement was no longer enough: "That's fine, Martin, but please, before you leave London and go on the boat, just write it all down in a fax for me. I need to know how I am going to live and have some sense of security."

No fax appeared. Instead, he called Len.

"Len, please talk some sense into Ilana; don't let her do anything stupid. I've bought her a house, and I will always take care of her."

"Martin, you need to take care of this directly with Ilana. I can't help you with this," Len replied.

Still no fax. You'd think that would be my first clue.

UNFINISHED BUSINESS

The next day, Martin flew from England to Italy to board the yacht. At first we spoke, but when I didn't hear from him for a couple of days, I decided not to call. I figured I would let him do his thing and stay out of the way. But we had some pending business to take care of. Immediately after breaking up with me, Martin, true to his word, had bought me a house. I would fix it up, and whenever I decided to sell, we'd split the profits. I was listed as the owner-occupier and it was my name on the loan documents, but the deed would be solely in *Martin's* name. The deal was in escrow, due to close on the following Monday. Martin was at sea, and he wasn't expected back until Wednesday.

Therefore, when the escrow officer called me on the Friday before and asked me to sign the papers, I held off. Martin's lawyer in Los Angeles, who had power of attorney, hadn't signed yet, so I instructed the escrow officer to send him the documents to sign first. I needed to speak to Martin before signing it myself.

Throughout our years together, I'd managed all our financial affairs but officially had no income or assets of my own. Nothing was under my name and, having retired from my business at Martin's request, I was financially dependent on him and would need his support until I could figure out my next move. Signing that escrow document would put me on the hook for a $7,000 monthly mortgage payment—money I did not have—and with zero income to boot. I'd always had great credit, and the idea of putting my signature on something with no idea of how I was going to pay for it left me feeling more than a little nervous and exposed. I had no reason to suspect that Martin wouldn't come through, as he promised to quitclaim the new house to me as soon as escrow closed, but my sister was adamant. She didn't like any of it.

"Ilana, you are not signing anything until Martin gets back," said Sharon.

"Don't be silly," I assured her. "I'll speak to him, and we'll sort this out. I know we will."

RADIO SILENCE

I called Martin over the weekend to get his assurance, planning to sign the papers on Monday. Unable to reach him, I left a message. A few hours later, another call. And another. No response. Nothing but radio silence. Had he drowned off the coast of Capri? I hadn't heard back from him all weekend, and it wasn't like him. During our years together we hadn't gone one day without speaking to each other. What was going on? Monday came, and so did a fax from Martin's lawyer.

"Martin really cares about you, but under the circumstances, could you please vacate the house by Wednesday," it said.

What circumstances? I wondered. It had to be some sick misunderstanding. I was still clinging to the belief that if I could just speak to Martin, this would all go away.

By now, Sharon was getting frantic.

"You can't just sit here like a fool, Ilana. For God's sake, speak to an attorney!"

Reluctantly, I made a couple of cold calls to attorneys. Making it clear that I had no money to cover legal fees and that whatever they did for me would have to be on a contingency basis did not deter them. It must have been something about the Patrón name, because some of the top celebrity attorneys in Los Angeles started courting me. Patrón's value had skyrocketed to $200 million-plus by then, so they figured there was money to be made from our misfortune. Why else would Tom Cruise's lawyer spend four hours on the phone dispensing free advice when I hadn't even agreed to retain him? Not that this sudden popularity was any comfort. It merely confirmed that something was terribly wrong.

SPECIAL DELIVERY

Several paranoia-inducing hours on the phone with those lawyers had put me on high alert. It's amazing what listening to worst-case scenarios can do to your head. But for all their differing opinions, the attorneys had one piece of advice that was consistent: under no circumstances was I to answer the door. "Speak to no one," they all said.

By eight-thirty Tuesday night, on my umpteenth phone call with a lawyer, I was a wreck. Someone buzzed at the gate, and without thinking I answered.

"Who's there?"

"Flower delivery for Ilana Edelstein."

I buzzed him in, and the lawyer of the minute on the line went berserk: "Are you insane? I can guarantee you that there are no flowers. That man has come to serve you papers!"

"What should I do?"

"Lock the doors and hide! Do not answer the door."

For the next several hours I stayed huddled inside our bedroom walk-in closet, the only room in the house without windows. When it was past midnight and the doorbell had long stopped ringing, I crept out of the closet and took a peak outside. No one was there, so I opened the door to a huge bouquet of beautiful flowers from Eloise, wishing me well. She knew about my breakup with Martin and was lending support.

I had to laugh. Those lawyers were making me crazy. They'd taken over before two people could be alone in a room together and talk. Martin was due home the next day. I just had to be patient until I could see him face to face. For a moment, I even allowed myself to believe that it really would be okay.

But Wednesday came and went, and Martin was a no-show. I went to his new offices in Montecito to find my gate clicker no longer worked, and when I rang the bell, the staff informed me they were forbidden to allow me entry.

I went to see Barry Cappello that night. We discussed how he would handle my case and what he'd need from me. Of all the lawyers I could have chosen to go with, Barry was the only one based in Santa Barbara, and that proximity gave me added comfort in my hour of need. So did the fact that he was recommended by my personal trainer and good friend Peter Park. Barry had been like a godfather to Peter, and for me that was a ringing endorsement.

Barry instructed me to go straight home and get to work photocopying every scrap of paper I could lay my hands on. By now, I was in a state of frenzy. My closest girlfriend, Nina, came by, and we spent the entire next day going through every file in the Windsong office. Our life together had come to this: a mountain of paper that could be used as fodder in a court case.

OPERATION PHOTOCOPY

There was still so much to do. Since my keys for the new Montecito office no longer worked, I called Miriam, our housekeeper at both properties, and asked her to leave a window unlocked so we could sneak in that Thursday night. She knew what was going on and was happy to oblige. We waited until Martin's office staff had gone home for the day, and then Nina and I snuck in and repeated the same photocopying exercise throughout the night. We had piles of paper that filled numerous boxes. I came home and collapsed. If I'd slept four hours in two days, it would have been a lot.

The next morning I intended to drop the papers off at Barry's offices, but because of the Windsong locksmith episode, Barry sent one of his staff to pick up the boxes. The rest of that morning was spent faxing back and forth with Barry, negotiating and signing our retainer agreement. My life was unraveling right before my eyes, and there was nothing I could do about it. I hated it. Our home, a veritable Garden of Eden, was fast becoming my own private hell. At least all that photocopying kept me busy and distracted enough not to drive myself crazy with speculation about what was really going on or what might happen next. But I soon had my answer.

Our breakup had spiraled out of control. We should have talked face to face alone. We should have remembered who we were and all that we meant to each other before allowing these so-called experts to fill our heads with suspicion and paranoia. But other people, namely, lawyers, got involved too much and too soon, turning tragic miscommunication into this bizarre cops and robbers scene.

Back in the kitchen, surrounded by all those men, I don't know what I would have done without Len. He was madly defending my honor, arguing with everyone and physically guarding me.

"Back off! Give her some goddamn space," he told them. "How dare you treat her this way? She hasn't done anything wrong!"

Dazed and confused, I picked myself up and headed to our bedroom to pack some bags. I had to collect myself, knowing I would need more than just a few overnight things. Once I left Windsong, there would be no going back. Reluctantly, I packed my personal belongings, realizing it would be the last time those walls would embrace me.

There was no question the kick-out order had somehow been obtained without due process. I'd never been served, and it was the first I'd heard of it. Evidently, Martin's lawyer stuck the paperwork under the judge's pen right before closing time. It was now five o'clock on a Friday afternoon, and the situation looked hopeless. All the courts were closed, and most judges in Santa Barbara would be out on the golf course by now. Justice would not be served.

Meanwhile, behind the scenes, Barry was working the phones. Thank God I'd chosen a local lawyer, because he knew everyone in the Santa Barbara court system and pulled off some stellar detective work to find out what was really going on. In his 40 years of practice, not once had he ever called a judge at home, but Barry somehow managed to track down this particular justice's number and call him:

"Your honor, I think you've made a grave mistake," he told him. "The sheriff is in her home, removing her as we speak. There's been no due process, she has never been served, and this is the first we've heard of this. I appeal to you; please correct this error."

"What do you want me to do?" the judge asked.

"Call the sheriff in her house right now and let's proceed lawfully."

The judge did call the sheriff and vacated the order.

STAY OF EXECUTION

The court had ordered that we both be allowed to stay at the house until the legal process took its proper course and established who would have to leave, at least a couple more weeks. Martin and I had become irrevocably estranged, yet somehow we would have to live under the same roof until the court decided our fate. Those two strangers I'd encountered trespassing on Windsong earlier that day were private investigators Martin had hired. They would have to live with us, in the house, around the clock, on Martin's dime, to "protect" him. If it had been someone else's life, I'd have laughed at the irony.

Martin stayed in one of the guesthouses, and during the next few days I was allowed to remain in the master suite and get my affairs in order. My time was spent collecting boxes and getting ready to leave even though I wasn't allowed to pack. We all knew who would eventually be leaving, but I couldn't let on because it might have suggested there was no claim against Martin, especially with the PIs around.

In the end, I was grateful for their presence. They turned out to be nice guys and were appreciative of my sharing imported English tea and food with them. I had no appetite and was certainly in no mood to entertain, but a guest in my home will always be treated with the utmost hospitality no matter what the circumstances. I was also glad I had someone there to bear witness to my composure in my darkest hours.

The vacated order bought me just enough time to regroup and find a place to land. Little did I realize that this ugly episode was only the first battle in a long and drawn out War of the Roses.

This wasn't the end. This was merely the beginning of the end.

STONE COLD SOBER

The morning after, in those gray moments between sleeping and waking, the previous day's drama felt like a bizarre nightmare. I'd barely slept, and in my fog I wondered, how could that have possibly been real? But when I padded into the kitchen to brew myself a cup of tea and saw the bodyguards sitting quietly at the table, there was no mistaking it.

As I was preparing coffee for the men, Martin appeared from one of the guesthouses.

"Ilana, can you please come outside? I need to speak to you."

"You can speak to me right here, Martin. After yesterday, God knows what I'll walk into next."

"I promise I just need to talk to you alone; please come outside," he insisted.

I followed him as he exited the kitchen and took position at the center of our huge motor courtyard. It was a glorious morning. The flowers were still covered in heavy drops of dew, the birds were chirping, and bees from my hive were humming. Everything around me was totally indifferent to this unfolding human catastrophe.

I waited for him to speak.

"Please, Ilana, let's not do this. Let's stop the madness and work this out together."

I just about choked. "Are you kidding me? Have you completely forgotten what happened here yesterday? And you seriously think I remotely trust you now? Besides, it's too late, Martin. Just yesterday morning I signed a retainer agreement with an attorney."

"Get rid of him; we can use my lawyer."

"You get rid of yours," I replied, "and we'll use mine. I'm on a contingency, so 30 percent goes to him no matter what."

The tragedy was that the train had already left the station. If we'd had that conversation a day earlier, who knows how it would have all turned out. I've often reflected on that and wondered if perhaps we could have changed course. I'll never know. In that moment, there didn't seem to be any way we could meet in the middle.

We'd lost ourselves in litigation. When relationships go sour, whether in love or in business, it's amazing what two people can do to tear each other apart, especially when third parties are involved. A partnership is a wonderful thing—until it isn't. That special chemistry between two people gets poisoned, and they are no longer recognizable to themselves or each other.

We were not the first, nor will we be the last, to engage in a bitter and soul-destroying fight that belied all that we meant to each other. In retrospect, it could have been resolved with the respect, compassion, and understanding we'd given each other throughout our relationship. Martin and I had always sworn we'd never travel down that road, especially after the Seagram's trial, yet here we were, just like any other angry, hurt couple going through an ugly divorce. We didn't have children, so Patrón, the thing we nurtured together, born of our love, became the object of our fierce battle even though I wasn't even trying to get custody.

It was my lawyer Barry's decision to plead the case as a breach of contract based on the fact that agreements, whether written or verbal, are binding and enforceable. Martin and I had verbally agreed we were partners in everything we did. Contrary to what most people assume, there is no common law in California, the most liberal state in the Union, so by no means was it a given that anything would be coming my way, and this case was way beyond a palimony suit. Since I strongly believed that compensation for my contribution to Patrón was due, confidence about proving it in court was building within me. When it came to my involvement, everyone knew exactly the role I'd played in developing the brand. My fastidiousness and years of business experience had established many details of the company and its operations. This was a battle I should have no problem winning.

PRIVILEGED INFORMATION

Perhaps I should have known better. When I met Barry later that morning to go over the details of what had happened and the case, his initial line of questioning completely threw me off.

"Do you do drugs?" he asked me.

Stunned, I answered, "Yes." It never occurred to me to lie; I had nothing to hide.

"What drugs?"

"I've done marijuana, coke, speed, and ecstasy. Why?"

"How often?"

"Socially, at parties. . . ."

"Are you addicted?"

"No."

"Are you high now?"

"No. Of course not. Barry, what's this all about? What on earth does my recreational drug use have to do with anything?"

In retrospect, I should not have been so honest. The fact was that once in a while I had indulged. As far as I was concerned, it was no one's business and totally unrelated to the issue at hand. "To each his own" has always been my motto. But the lawyers saw otherwise. They were seeking to detract from the facts of our business agreement and thereby attempting to diminish my significance and credibility. These damaging and humiliating allegations would be scandalous to the conservative Santa Barbara judge and jury.

Of course I was not a drug addict and was damned if I was going to be intimidated into defending myself as one. The fact was that after 13 years of building the business of Patrón alongside him, I was certainly entitled to something. To counter this claim, I was being portrayed as nothing more than a piece of arse bought and paid for. These lawyers seemed hell-bent on proving that for all those years I was there just for drugs and sex and that any notion that I was involved with Patrón was just a by-product of my delusions.

There was no rationale as to what the judge allowed or disallowed to be presented in court. He seemed partial to the sex and drug theme, which continued throughout the three-month trial. I seriously questioned the judge's rulings on evidence that was very relevant to the case and not allowed to be presented to the jury. I had piles of documentation authenticating my role in everything, including the company, but wasn't permitted to use them as evidence on the grounds that they were "prejudicial." Included on that list were the loan documents for the house that Martin was buying for me after we split up, naming me as owner and occupier. My stated income and ownership of assets were also included in the paperwork, regardless of the fact that I had no income and Windsong was owned by a corporation. It was indisputable proof that I was more than just some drug-addled nymphomaniac in his bedroom. There also were documents naming me as Patrón's corporate secretary.

BOOB GATE

Parts of the proceedings verged on the farcical. My best friend, Nina, did take the stand. She was our lead Patrón Girl and a blonde bombshell who'd come to the United States from Norway years ago as a nanny, fallen in love with California, and never left.

Nina shared my European sensibilities and wicked sense of humor. She was highly intelligent, very personable, and grasped the uniqueness of Patrón from the moment she tasted it. Martin and I both recognized her potential as a brand ambassador. She was someone we could rely on to run an event without us having to be there to hold her hand, and we sent her all over the world in that capacity. Conversely, when we traveled, Nina would house sit for us at Windsong and take care of our pets and property, so she certainly knew us on every level, both personally and professionally.

True to form, Martin's lawyers only exploited the personal. They attempted to use Nina to demonstrate how our life was nothing but sex orgies and that she was one of the regular participants.

"Didn't you eat dinner at Windsong every night?" Patty Glaser, a member of Martin's legal team, asked her.

"Not every night, but regularly."

"Isn't it true there were wild sex parties filled with drugs?"

"Not when I was there."

Among the many things Nina and I had in common was a cosmopolitan casualness about nudity. As a South African, I'd always sunbathed topless, as did Nina, and we regularly did so at our pool. Nina had also attended many parties at Windsong that occasionally ended up with a skinny-dip in the pool in the wee hours of the morning. But as far as we were concerned, nudity was not to be confused with sex. It was natural, beautiful, and perfectly harmless. Martin's lawyers, in a big attempt to catch her in a lie that would permit them to introduce new innocent and personal photographs, tried their best to suggest otherwise.

"No sex, Ms. Svele? Well, what about this?"

Up on the huge screen flashed a picture of a bunch of girls topless in our Jacuzzi. It was bigger than life, showing steam rising past a varied assortment of nipples, Nina's among them. This picture happened to be taken at a bachelorette party I hosted for a girlfriend at which we all ended up naked in the hot tub. It was all women, except for Martin, who was allowed to stay on condition that he tended the bar. He was always one of the girls anyway, so his presence was comfortable for everyone. That picture was one of many that he took that night.

"Ms. Svele, are these your breasts?" inquired Glaser, tapping that part of the picture with a telescoping pointer.

"Yes, those would be my boobs," Nina said in a comically thick Scandinavian accent.

Her delivery had the courtroom in stitches. Thank God Nina had a sense of humor about it all. I don't know what I would have done without her.

Months after the trial, several attorneys living in Santa Barbara who were familiar with the case shared their utter disbelief at the way the judge handled it. One prevailing theory was that the elderly white male adjudicator couldn't get past his shock at my alleged lifestyle and the scandalous fact that Martin and I were living together without being married. In his eyes, I was a fallen floozy. Perhaps he wasn't horrified as much as titillated. Why else would he keep circling back to all this irrelevant detail?

SIMPLE QUESTIONS

The Patrón employees and associates who were called in as witnesses hardly seemed to matter in the case. We had all of five staff members, including an office manager, an assistant, our sales and marketing team, and a chief financial officer. I'd interviewed and hired most of them myself. In the end, their testimony didn't hurt my case. They knew nothing about my personal life, and the few times the attorneys asked factual questions about the business and my role in the operations—everything from running the finances, to marketing and promotions, to developing and maintaining the company website— they answered truthfully.

"Who hired you?"

"Ilana."

"Who trained you?"

"Ilana."

"Was there any one person that you believed had comprehensive knowledge of all aspects of your office and the business?"

"Ilana."

The overall effect of John Paul's testimony was also neutral; it didn't help or hurt either side. I was mortified that he had to be involved at all. It was a huge imposition to ask him to fly in to testify. My suit was in no way a threat to the future of Patrón. If I had won the trial, it would not have hurt his interest in any way. But you never know what a lawyer will ask.

Throughout the trial I barely saw Martin, much less spoke to him. I have no idea what was going through his mind or how much the court proceedings were a runaway train beyond his control. But I caught a glimpse on the day he took the stand, when his lawyer seemed hell-bent on distorting our domestic arrangement.

"Mr. Crowley, tell us about your sex life with the plaintiff. Did you have threesomes involving other women?"

"Oh, yes; many times," Martin replied proudly. "It was beautiful."

"Was Ms. Edelstein on drugs at the time in order to be able to cope with you being with another woman? Wasn't she in the way? Did you want her there at all?"

The questions were gifts. The lawyer was trying to give Martin every opportunity to say I was of no significance to him, but Martin refused to succumb to a lie even if it helped his case.

"Absolutely not! She didn't need drugs. It was what she and I both wanted equally and together."

"But she was nothing to you and you feared for your life. Isn't that right, Mr. Crowley? When was the last time you had sex with the plaintiff?"

"A month ago."

The legal eagle's jaw dropped; then his glasses fell off his nose. He couldn't believe how much his client was putting his foot in it. For a brief moment, their perverse tactics during this seemingly endless legal farce were beginning to backfire.

Despite the emotional turmoil I was going through, my own testimony went well. There wasn't a single fact about the details of the business I couldn't answer or describe, and my team covered them all. Of course, the number of questions regarding my role in Patrón was frustratingly few from the other side.

It was without a doubt the darkest period of my life. I'd lost my greatest love and the sense of purpose that had driven me for more than a decade. The irony was that the very thing that connected us all these years, Patrón, became a catalyst for this bloody battle. Had it not grown into a liquor behemoth, perhaps none of this would have happened. The business was booming, with sales consistently doubling year after year. Our breakup became ugly because too much was at stake. Patrón, the very thing that had been emblematic of our relationship and the magical world we created together, became our undoing as lovers.

VICTOR'S SPOILS

In the end, my case was lost on a technicality. The jury unanimously believed I was entitled to a reward, but they were not in a position to say how much. The case had been bifurcated, meaning it would be tried in two completely separate trials. The first trial was purely to establish whether I was due something, and no amounts or percentages were to be addressed. If at the end of the trial it was found that I was due something, there'd be a second trial, complete with a new jury, to establish the amount of the award.

In retrospect, my lawyers pleaded the case wrong. Never for a moment did I believe I was due the 50 percent they were asking for. I only wanted whatever was fair to both sides on the basis of my contribution to the business. But my team had somehow convinced me that it was all part of a strategy from which we could negotiate to come up with what would probably have been a much lower sum. It gave the opposing counsel an opening. In her closing statements, Martin's attorney ranted, "Ladies and gentlemen of the jury, this woman is going after 50 percent of everything this man owns."

Suddenly, out of nowhere a number was thrown out to the jury under the guise of closing statements, when no objections are allowed. After one and a half days of deliberation, the confused jury members sent a note to the judge, asking if they were to take into account the 50 percent factor. The judge finally sent a reply instructing them to consider all the facts presented when making their decision. Five minutes later they emerged with their verdict.

Martin won.

Ultimately, the real victors were the lawyers. As in any litigation case, the plaintiffs are no more than pawns in an expensive game run by men and women more interested in winning than in having justice served. The opposing attorneys make their fortunes through adversarial relationships, and somehow they've monetized this personal pain and conflict. There were strong grounds for appeal, but truth be told, the rancor of those legal proceedings ate into my soul. I just couldn't do it anymore.

CHAPTER 8

Loose Ends

His complexion was gray, his shoulders were hunched over, and he sat there like a little old man. It was the first time in two years I'd seen Martin outside of a courtroom, and I was shocked at how he looked. Everything about his demeanor signaled unhappiness. Despite the nastiness of our trial, my heart sank and I felt a wave of compassion. I could never be with Martin again, but I'd never stopped caring.

We were meeting at Windsong. Martin was packing the place up and putting everything, including my belongings, into storage because he was going to live on a newly acquired megayacht based in Monte Carlo.

Days before, with a fractured soul and no clue about how I'd be received, I'd called Martin, thinking we needed to talk in person.

"What do you want to talk about?" he asked.

"I have no idea; we just need to talk."

Face to face, there was a lot to be said. This was my chance to try to make sense of all the madness. Here he was, packing all my things away in boxes. Just a few months earlier, that sight would have rendered me irate. But suddenly it ceased to matter. Refusing to do this anymore, I just wanted out. The lawyers were the only ones who benefited at the expense of our souls. Every fiber of my being had been consumed by this for over two years. Now I was done and no longer gave a damn. The second that choice was made, I felt the shift. All that stuff was meaningless. Having lived without it for so long, there was nothing I needed anymore.

But first, there was one burning question:

"I didn't come here to rehash everything we've been through. But what I would really like to know is what it was that I did that made you turn on me. Because I sure as hell don't want to do that to anyone ever again."

"You didn't do anything," he replied.

"Then why?"

"Just followed my attorneys' orders. They kept telling me what you could have done."

"But was I doing any of those things?"

"No, you weren't," he said. "So what do you need?"

"Nothing. The way you've been clinging to everything, you apparently need it more than I. Keep it."

We spoke about his life since the trial, which, by his description, appeared to be void of joy.

"Do you have anyone in your life?"

"No," he said. "I'm grossly lonely, grossly unhappy, and grossly sick."

REDEMPTION

And he was. It was April 2003, almost two years since we'd last seen each other in that courtroom. I was busy rebuilding my life and livelihood, starting up a new financial consulting business from scratch, and was fast approaching the level of clients I'd had before retiring at Martin's request. I was returning to the things I enjoyed before Martin was in my life: dancing, spending lots of quality time with my family, dating here and there (although nothing serious), running my own successful company, and getting paid for my efforts. But Martin had no personal life to speak of. As often happens when couples split, friends chose sides, and he had few people left in his circle. Yet something in his demeanor hinted at a desire to turn things around.

Our old friend Caroline Law confirmed this, at least in part. She and Tom had essentially cut Martin out of their lives during the trial, and he was the last person Caroline wanted to hear from when Martin called them out of the blue in late February, just a couple of months before my meeting with him. It so happened that Tom was in an advanced stage of cancer and about to undergo grueling treatments. The news sparked a compassion and concern in Martin that blew her away. Caroline felt the genuine warmth of friendship return as Martin questioned her about Tom's health. Tom was too sick to speak with Martin directly, so Martin asked her to pass on a message: "Tell him he has to make it through these treatments, because you're both joining me on my new yacht and coming to Europe."

Tom and Martin both loved sailing. It was the carrot that got Tom through the weeks of agony. Then, in March, while waiting for one of his radiation treatments, Tom picked up a sailing magazine from the waiting room table. He opened it, and there was a two-page spread featuring the boat Martin had just bought. Tom took it as a sign and looked at that picture every day for the next six weeks. It became the dream he clung to, and having something like that surely gave him the will to live and contributed to his recovery. For that, Tom and Caroline will be forever grateful to Martin.

In retrospect, Tom's situation moved Martin at a time when he was facing his own mortality. The two men were the same age, they had known each other for 16 years, and Martin was about as close to Tom as he was to any man. Over the last few years Martin's health had deteriorated to such a degree that he needed a heart transplant. While we were still together, his cardiologist and lifesaver through-out the years, Dr. Robert Siegel, repeatedly encouraged him to have a defibrillator implanted in his chest, but Martin flat out refused. Then, just months after we separated, his condition declined so rapidly that he didn't have a choice and was forced to have the procedure. He was precluded from getting on any waiting list for a heart because of his overall health and lifestyle; he was not a candidate for a transplant. In desperation, he reached out to John Paul, a man who has always been fastidious about his own health. JP was shocked when he saw him.

"Martin, you don't look so good," he said.

"No, JP, I'm dying. I'm in desperate need of a heart transplant but don't qualify. Is there anything you can do to help advance me onto the heart transplant list?"

"Oh, my God, Martin, this really is bad; of course I will help you."

Though they were still very much partners in Patrón, their rela-tionship had been cool for the last two or three years, but John Paul still cared about his old friend and would help him any way he could. He put Martin up in his Beverly Hills mansion, where he could enjoy peace and quiet away from everything. JP got him into med-itation. Then he pulled some strings and got Martin in to see one of the most sought after cardiologists in the world, his friend Dr. Dean Ornish, who immediately put Martin on a strict diet and health regimen. Martin followed it religiously for a few months and began to regain some of his old vitality. It was a miraculous turnaround, to be sure.

EVERYTHING TO
LIVE FOR

Things were finally improving for Martin, and business was better than ever. After the ordeal with Seagram's, he made the decision to take over the warehousing and distribution of Patrón. It was one of the best decisions he ever made, increasing the profit margin and giving him control of the brand again, putting him in a position to respond to whatever the Patrón market demanded. They were finally in charge of their own destiny. The company was soaring. Bacardi had already approached Martin; talks ensued, initiating their quest to acquire Patrón. A bona fide offer was made while Martin and I were still together. It became apparent that the company needed to be corporatized in order to really have something to sell.

The success continued long after we separated, and Martin was becoming wealthy beyond his wildest dreams. All that he'd worked toward was finally coming to fruition. On paper at least, he had everything to live for. Then he went off the rails. True to form, Martin was in denial about his heart condition and had a short memory when it came to his health. Feeling invincible, he slipped back into his old ways. When I saw him that last time, the damage already had been done. His physical decline had been rapid; I had never seen him in worse shape.

The day after our meeting at Windsong, Martin's gardener showed up at my little rented house in Montecito and unloaded from his small truck a television set, some art objects, my photo albums, and all my arts and crafts supplies that Martin had no use for. I'd like to believe that he actually felt bad and was attempting to make amends.

LAST LAUGH

During that meeting, Martin told me he was flying to Anguilla the next day. The best kept secret in the Caribbean, this magical British West Indies island was the Patrón corporation's domicile as well as Pyrat Rum's blending, aging, and bottling plant.

The fact that he was traveling in that condition perturbed me. "Martin, you shouldn't be flying anywhere right now," I offered. "Why would you jeopardize your health to that degree?"

"People are depending on me," he said. "I can't let them down."

It was no longer my place to monitor his health. Unlike the old days, when I was the one who made sure we had enough of all his medications to last through our trips, he had no one. If it was left to Martin, it would inevitably result in a mad scramble to track down Dr. Siegel, who would then overnight us an adequate supply. I was also the one most likely to detect when his heart was out of rhythm. In spite of everything that had happened between us in the recent past, I was still concerned, so I called Martin in Anguilla on several occasions to check up on him. He seemed grateful and comforted by our conversations, which he'd prolong as much as he could. It was apparent that both of us embraced being able to talk to each other again, almost as if we were slowly and tentatively rebuilding the friendship we'd once had.

On one of the calls, after expressing relief that I would no longer appeal the case, he surprised me and said, "I want you to know you don't need to worry. At the end of the day you will have the last laugh."

I had been wondering if I was still the beneficiary in his wills but could never bring myself to ask. It was as if he had read my mind. I took his comment to mean that he hadn't changed a thing and that I remained his sole heir. I couldn't help but think this was Martin's way of reassuring me. But it was to be the last conversation we had.

The next day, Martin was at home in Anguilla when he suffered a massive coronary and fell down a flight of stairs. He was found by the security guard early the next morning. The man who lived high on a hill at the center of attention had died alone at the bottom of a staircase. It was hardly a fitting end for someone who was larger than life.

I was gutted. Although we were no longer a couple, it was a tremendous loss and I truly felt like his widow. Until that point he had been the most important person in my life. Whatever our recent history, he was still the love of my life, a fact that his lawyers did their utmost to destroy and expunge from the record.

CONFUSING LEGACY

Historically, there were in fact two handwritten wills: one for his American holdings, which included little but our Windsong estate, which had been heavily mortgaged to finance the Polish vodka factory, and the other for Martin's Anguillan offshore assets, which included his share of Patrón. But apparently he had changed his mind. A new typewritten document was to cover all his assets. According to this document, Martin left everything to educate underprivileged children.

The net effect of the will was that half of the Patrón business was now under the control of Martin's estate. I briefly considered contesting the will, but as we were never married, it was more than likely a court would have determined that Martin's assets should go to his next of kin. Clearly, that was not a fight in which I was going to engage.

I hadn't seen Martin's family in years. Then, in June 2003, I saw them for the last time at his memorial service in Los Angeles. I was deeply moved by the concern and love of Jon Crowley, who was stricken by the loss of his older brother. He was desperate to talk with someone who knew Martin, and he was angry and hurt that Martin had never let him in.

"Ilana, I believe one of the reasons he pushed people away was because they knew the truth and he didn't want anyone to really know him. If that happened, he would be real and imperfect like the rest of humanity."

"You may have a point, Jon," I told him. That may well have been part of the reason I was pushed away. We'll never know.

A week later, Jon wrote me a letter:

> I want you to know the moment we shared at Martin's memorial service will always be special and remind me of that day. You are the only person I have still cried with. I have tried to figure that out. I really needed to cry, so for whatever reason thank you for being there. Ilana, you were there when Martin had nothing and needed help. . . . You are the only reason we had any closeness to Martin. You brought our family and Martin together. That is priceless.

The written acknowledgment of my role in Martin's life was enough. I no longer had a dog in this fight.

FINAL BATTLE

But John Paul did. Learning his lesson from his partnership with the late Paul Mitchell, JP and Martin had signed a buy-sell agreement in 1996 that gave them each first right of refusal to buy the other's 50 percent should one of them die. Upon Martin's death, JP immediately exercised his right, so all that remained was to establish the price. His initial offer, in the low eight digits, was far below what the company was worth, bearing in mind Bacardi's offer two years before and that didn't include all the products, only Patrón. The trustees refused his offer, which from their fiduciary duty standpoint was the right thing to do.

Among other things, the agreement didn't adequately provide for the valuation of shares. The result was that JP's option to buy was now in doubt, and Bacardi was ready to step in and buy Martin's 50 percent from the trustees of his estate. An unsolicited corporate takeover by Bacardi seemed almost imminent and was unwelcome, to say the least.

The trustees took their case to court in Anguilla, the jurisdiction of Patrón's world headquarters, to determine whether the agreement between Martin and JP could be upheld. The court duly declared the agreement invalid, so JP took it to the British courts, where he appealed the Anguillan ruling.

As this process drew out over the next five years, Patrón's sales went stratospheric. Thanks to the solid foundation Martin had laid, the leadership of John Paul, and the crack marketing team he appointed, the brand had become hotter than ever. In addition, Martin's move to cut out the middleman and handle distribution and warehousing in-house, along with the decision to build a new Patrón factory with greater capacity and efficiency, meant there was enough product to meet consistent and growing consumer demand. Patrón's supply problems were well in the past. It meant that the company was worth far more than Bacardi's original offer to Martin for only the Patrón portion of the business.

CHESS MASTER

Patrón's revenues would consistently rise, as they had been doing since the birth of the business. JP and I kept in touch throughout all of this, and at one of my visits to his Malibu estate, we were catching up on the events in our lives when it suddenly occurred to me what was naturally happening. I shook my head and with a big smile said: "Wow, JP; I just got it. The longer this all remains in court, the closer you get to Patrón's other half paying for itself, based on how sales have been multiplying every year."

Smiling like a Cheshire cat, his reply was something along the lines of: "You got that right, Ilana."

But while the appeal was still in process, Bacardi made the trustees an offer of $175 million contingent on the outcome in the British courts. If the trustees were free of their obligation to JP and able to sell Martin's half to whoever they wanted, they could close that chapter and proceed with funding Martin's Windsong Trust, which they had set up to educate underprivileged children around the world. Of course they accepted, and it shook JP to his core. There was a very real danger he could lose this battle, so in January 2007 he brought out the big guns, offering the trustees $755 million for Martin's half, which of course they were thrilled to accept. There was just one problem: they had already accepted Bacardi's first offer. Bacardi immediately filed an injunction in the Anguilla court to stop the sale, insisting the trustees had already accepted a fair offer.

BusinessWeek magazine's account of this struggle for control of Patrón described it as a "barroom brawl."[1] Hardly. It was more like a high-stakes chess game, and JP was its Garry Kasparov, playing out each move with the patience and strategic skills of a grandmaster. I stood on the sidelines throughout, rooting for him to win. To my great relief, it wasn't my battle this time, but I knew it would have been Martin's wish to leave Patrón in the hands of the one man who loved and understood the brand as much as we did. It was JP's baby just as much as it was ours, and he'd been right there with us, nurturing the brand from the moment it was born. No one deserved control of the company more.

Another year went by, again to JP's benefit, as Patrón revenues continued to soar. Ever the smooth negotiator, JP eventually went directly to Bacardi and made them an offer for a minority stake that they gladly accepted. He also offered an undisclosed amount to the charity set up by Martin's estate. It was JP's ingenious way of making everyone happy in the end.

EVERYONE WINS

In July 2008, JP and Bacardi announced the deal for an "unspecified" minority stake in the company. Bacardi's vice chairman, Barry Kabalkin, was given a seat on the board, and JP became the principal owner.

In his press statement, JP announced: "Martin and I shared a commitment to help those in need of assistance throughout the world, and I'm pleased to say that implementation of this agreement will make a truly meaningful difference to those who deserve it most. The company has done extremely well, due in large part to our outstanding team of employees, and we have an incredible opportunity to build upon that success with Bacardi."

Ready to make nice, Bacardi's chairman, Facundo Bacardi, had his own kind words to say: "John Paul DeJoria and the late Martin Crowley are to be congratulated for creating an extraordinary, handcrafted product and achieving its enormous success in the marketplace—and for their contribution to the growth of the Tequila industry overall. We look forward to this new relationship and to working together."

JP had won, and as a result, so had Patrón. Although I was no longer part of the business, it mattered to me deeply that Martin's legacy would be left under the best possible stewardship. Unfettered by the problems of the past, Patrón was now poised for a level of growth beyond Martin's wildest imagination. Our baby's future was assured.

CHAPTER 9

Patrón Today

A FEW YEARS AGO I received a phone call from a man claiming to represent a certain celebrity. This unspecified famous person, I was told, was interested in procuring a tequila brand, and he'd somehow heard that I might know where to find a factory that made only the best. His client had the wherewithal to reward me generously for any introductions I made on his behalf.

It so happened that I did know of such a place. The original factory that had produced the tequila for Patrón had stopped supplying as a result of a falling out with Martin. Ten years after the fact, they'd learned that he'd registered the worldwide rights to their original name and never told them. Martin and I discussed this extensively over the years. Notwithstanding the fact that Martin had made them wealthy beyond their wildest dreams, they were pissed. They'd had many differences over the years, but this particular omission had done irreparable damage to Martin's relationship with them. I could see it from both sides. What Martin did was a sound business move. He didn't want to take the chance of this family putting a rival to Patrón on the market. But he should have told them at the time. Out of sheer spite, they stopped supplying Patrón.

The way top-shelf tequila has taken off as a brand category, this factory could do very well with the right marketing and backing. They make a sublime tequila the old-fashioned way. But not only was I not about to do that to Patrón, my journey with tequila was long over. Besides, I didn't like all the secrecy over the identity of this interested party.

"Why on earth would I want to do business with someone who won't even identify himself?" I told this celebrity's middle man.

"His name is P. Diddy."

"Oh. Then please tell Mr. Combs that if he is genuinely interested, he should call me himself, because I do not do business through third parties."

The fact was that my journey in the tequila business ended the day Martin and I separated. My only connection to Patrón today is as an informed observer and ardent fan, so I never seriously entertained the possibility of a deal with a rap mogul.

But Patrón's connection with hip-hop, which was not on our radar in the early years, did intrigue me. A couple of years later, when Mr. Combs's name popped up in a conversation I was having with John Paul about Patrón's influence across various cultures, his reaction took me somewhat by surprise:

"Oh, yeah; he's my buddy. Puffy and I are good friends."

NEW HORIZONS

As it turns out, JP has become close with many other major figures in the music and hip-hop world who adore the brand, including Cee Lo Green and Snoop Lion (formerly Snoop Dogg). He has even joined forces with them through various philanthropic missions, such as

Snoop Lion's involvement in the Mind Garden Project in Jamaica to help underprivileged families plant more gardens.

Hip-hop is a community that has embraced Patrón as its drink of choice, even rhyming about the brand in its music. JP informed me that to date, Patrón had been mentioned in about 200 songs, including rap, pop, and country, although the majority of references appear in hip-hop music. As artists and performers of this genre have matured and become more successful and sophisticated across various industries, their devotion to the brand has intensified.

Patrón has come to symbolize a lifestyle of all the finest things in life to which one can aspire, and that's powerful in a culture that prizes success. Just as we didn't pay for product placement in Hollywood movies in the early days, those musical references to Patrón happened completely organically, by sheer virtue of the quality of the product and the loyalty of its diverse fans. This open architecture marketing style went against everything taught at the finest business schools in the country. "Identify and target your audience to market efficiently" is their motto. But it never made sense to Martin or me to narrow our audience.

I don't profess to have much personal knowledge of what goes on in the hip-hop community aside from the music, least of all their libation of choice. But when I happened to mention that I was chronicling the early years of the story of Patrón to the simply delicious Daymond John, an entrepreneur with deep roots in the world of rap and the star of the ABC hit show *Shark Tank*, he graciously offered to educate me on hip-hop's significant connection to the brand: "It works because it's organic. When we first came across Patrón, it felt like a noncommercial brand. It wasn't necessarily marketed to us; it was adopted by us, and people like that sense of discovery."

Daymond should know. He is a marketing maven with a particular genius for understanding what the customer wants. From the streets of Queens, New York, he started one of the world's most successful urban clothing labels, FUBU, which earned about $400 million in sales at its peak.

As he tells it, the hip-hop world's discovery of Patrón began while Martin was still alive. Daymond first came across Patrón in 2001 in New Orleans at a recording session under his music label for the hip-hop producer Lil Jon, whom he represents. Never a fan of tequila, Daymond was struck by how different it was: "I used to be a waiter at Red Lobster, so Cuervo was the only brand I knew. But Patrón tasted much better to me. Like nothing else, in fact."

Lil Jon was and is an eccentric character, known at the time for his long dreadlocks, gold teeth, and monosyllabic catchphrases. But he was also a highly influential and prolific music producer and tastemaker, and fans across cultures were following his lead on everything from what music to enjoy to which sneakers to buy. By being so visible at parties, at press events, and in videos with his ever present Patrón bottle, he helped to establish our brand in the urban youth market.

After some further research, I learned that Patrón references permeate the hip-hop culture. There was a time when Grammy-winning music producer Jermaine Dupri famously drank only Patrón at the many industry parties he attended. Patrón appeared in a video by the pop star Usher, one of Dupri's musical protégés, and in countless others. There was even an entire song dedicated to the brand: "Patrón Tequila" by the Paradiso Girls, a quintet of sexy young women reminiscent of the Pussycat Dolls.

AUTHENTIC APPEAL

The fact of Patrón's deep and diverse market penetration was obvious. But I was more interested in why.

"People feel more of a connection to Patrón than to other brands," Daymond explained. "The tastemakers found something they feel everyone should be part of. As its market broadened, Patrón already had a core consumer base that says, 'I was on to that first.'"

There is something about the authenticity of Patrón that appeals to the most discerning consumers. Because it came along before all the other tequilas tried to go high-end, it is regarded as the "official brand," versus something that was manufactured for a specific market. And of course, once the awareness is created, the superior taste solidifies a fiercely loyal customer base.

This fact played out a few years ago when a new tequila brand was launched through the hit television series *Entourage*, a show with a strong youth following. The writers of the program, presumably in concert with this particular tequila company's owner, manufactured a story line that sounded remarkably similar to our own: an obscure high-quality tequila gets "discovered" in a remote corner of Mexico and brought to the Los Angeles scene by one of the characters on the show. It was certainly clever, and imitation is the sincerest form of flattery. But in my opinion, true tequila connoisseurs know the difference.

Influential consumers appreciate a brand that builds naturally, through word of mouth and educated connoisseurs. That is how we established ourselves from the beginning, without ever going after any one particular market segment. When you create something that is sublime, there is no need to chase.

"The easiest thing to sell is the truth," Daymond explained.

Other brands have tried, and that's precisely the problem. The urban youth market has become hugely important to the liquor industry, with many companies going out of their way to create products that appeal just to this group. Multinational corporations dedicate millions of marketing dollars to be identified with all things cool. But it's tricky, because this is an audience with a built-in radar for insincerity, and trying too hard can frequently backfire.

In rare instances, this more contrived approach can work. The liquor giant Diageo threw millions of dollars behind Ciroc Vodka by making Mr. Combs their spokesman and giving him equity in the brand. To get ahead in a market with so many other vodkas, it was a successful and intelligent gambit, as Ciroc is now the company's bestselling brand. Mr. Combs has been an excellent spokesman for the brand, with sleek rat-pack-themed television ads. But the emphasis on elegance, sophistication, and celebrating responsibly is nothing new. We've been doing it for years.

DIFFERENT YET THE SAME

Capturing the urban youth market is just one of the many ways in which the brand has evolved since Martin died, yet at the same time it's truly a result of what Patrón has always been: a brand that never targeted any one particular market. We were always about maintaining consistently high standards, not compromising on quality, as well as having fun.

But the time was ripe for Patrón's marketing and distribution strategies to morph in recognition of its global status as a brand. It wasn't going to be business as usual, and growing pains were becoming apparent. Change is never easy.

It began with the leadership. I was present when Martin had interviewed and hired Ed Brown, a former top executive at Seagram's, as Patrón's head of sales, and he struck me as a sharp man with vast experience in many areas of consumer brand marketing. At Seagram's, Ed had been in charge of $5 billion in sales for the Asia-Pacific region, based in Singapore. He came to us from the big leagues and knew of other approaches that might help as we entered a new phase of growth. But Martin still remained the decision maker.

I subsequently learned from JP that this management style was a source of constant tension between JP and Martin in those final two years. At issue was Martin's insistence on using sexy Playmates in the ad campaigns. It had worked well for many years, but others felt that it was time for a fresh approach. There's value in doing what always worked in the past, but one should know the difference between consistency and clinging to the old ways.

A NEW REGIME

When JP took over all the decision making for the business after Martin died, he and Ed put an immediate stop to the Bunnies and made Patrón the hero of its own print campaigns with the tagline "Simply Perfect," featuring beautifully shot portraits of the bottles themselves. The busty Patrón Girls became obsolete. Now at promotions you are more likely to see a clean-cut young man serving up a sample of the brand. Personally, I miss the girls, but I understand that it's necessary to adapt to the times.

Martin had done extraordinarily well building the business from nothing. It's amazing how much he was able to execute all those years. There were fewer than a dozen employees at the end of his reign, and he held himself accountable for every single aspect of the business. When Bacardi approached him with the buy offer, he realized that what they would be buying was him and that had to change immediately. Until then, the business had never had a corporate structure; Martin had handled everything: production, sales, marketing, finance, and so on. A more formal framework was desperately needed, so he began the process of departmentalizing by seeking to hire the best in the field to set up and run each department. It was a slow process, and Martin wasn't used to delegating.

JP's particular strength lies in finding the best and trusting his people. With a full stake in the business, he brought a fresh enthusiasm and perspective to Patrón, not to mention resources. He hired a whole new team, many of whom also came from the executive ranks of Seagram's, which became defunct in 2000. Under Ed Brown, now president and CEO, Patrón suddenly had whole departments dedicated to promotions, marketing, social media, and sales.

The goal was to increase market penetration. Whereas we had sold across the country and in a handful of international markets, Ed and JP wanted Patrón to be everywhere, and rightly so. They started fortifying their distribution team, making sure Patrón was available everywhere on and off premise in every bar, restaurant, and retail location. The only thing that was stopping even further growth in sales was lack of availability, but that soon changed. Its sales and distribution were fortified in keeping with the needs of a truly global brand. Early in 2012, it made further inroads into new markets in Asia, the Pacific, Europe, the Middle East, and Latin America.

In fact, East Asia is now Patrón's fastest-growing market, with sales in the region having increased by 82 percent in 2011.[1] The sales team has been pushing hard to build Patrón's presence in travel retail outlets, including the duty-free shops at Tokyo's Narita Airport as well as in South Korea, Cambodia, and Taiwan, countries where brown spirits have traditionally dominated. Today, Patrón is sold in 130 airports and 700 duty-free outlets around the world.

Now, Patrón is sold in more than 120 countries, with global distributors from Andorra to Zimbabwe. Patrón's products, which now include Ultimat Vodka, Citronge Orange Liqueur, and variously aged categories of Pyrat Rum and Patrón are everywhere. Fans from Kiev to Helsinki judge the quality of their local bars by whether the brand is available. Patrón is even sold in Mexico, which ironically had not been the case during Martin's guidance, because he wanted to avoid having Patrón fall victim to the gray market, which was prevalent in Mexico at the time.

From what I have seen, Patrón has been doing what it had always been doing to increase coverage and exposure, but multiplied by a factor of 100 under this new regime. Everything is done to a much bigger scale. Whereas JP had offered bottles of Patrón at the occasional John Paul Mitchell trade show and events in the past, since 2004 Patrón has been prominently featured at all of his biggest gatherings in Las Vegas, which are attended by as many as 3,000 top hairstylists from around the world. Ice bars are set up, samples are given away, and Patrón branding festoons these huge events. Of course it's a win-win for John Paul. He makes his best customers from his other business ventures feel special, and they in turn become roving ambassadors for and consumers of the brand.

ALL CYLINDERS

All the extra things that Patrón should have been doing were finally being done, and how. In 2006, Patrón made advertising industry news with a $25 million campaign budget, representing a 150 percent increase in ad spending and making it one of the liquor industry's top spenders, up there with Grey Goose and Bacardi, according to *Advertising Age*. Included in that budget was $5 million for Patrón's first-ever television spots. That kind of investment was inconceivable when Martin was alive.

The push continued in 2007, when Patrón became an early adopter of corporate social media with the establishment of the Patrón Social Club. A members-only site for Patrón enthusiasts offering exclusive cocktail recipes, special event access, and a kind of pirate dining society for discerning foodies and mixologists who subscribe to the site, the club is designed to build a sense of community among Patrón enthusiasts. Exclusive cocktail recipes, special menu pairings, and breathtaking dining experiences are made even more memorable as members answer riddles to unlock the secret location of the next Patrón rendezvous. In addition to information about Patrón, it includes a section called "ID Your Bottle" so that members can find out the origins of one of the individually numbered bottles and learn which field the agave was grown in and the year it was harvested, bottled, and distilled to further enhance their sense of personal connection to the brand.

The Patrón Social Club included print, television, and billboards, with the tagline "Some perfection is debatable. Some is not." The idea was to invite consumers to voice their opinions about Patrón and its entire product range. But the website does more than any two-dimensional messaging can by building up a customer list and strengthening loyalty among existing buyers of the brand. It invites members to create a customer profile, asking them questions about fashion, nightlife, and their favorite bars so that Patrón can personalize its marketing efforts to make them feel special with events, sweepstakes, and products aimed just at them. It's a personal census beyond compare in the industry. As happy customers, they become the best advocates for the brand.

I can't help but think how much faster Patrón would have grown in the early days if we'd had access to such sophisticated online marketing. Then again, perhaps if we'd gone viral too soon, it would have killed that sense of exclusivity. Perhaps, like Patrón itself, our particular magic in those early years resulted from a slow and careful process of cultivation and reinforcement. Either way, the decision to launch the Patrón Social Club is a brilliant extension of the kind of social experience Martin and I tried to create before social media were available—a variation on a theme, if you will. But somehow we still managed to reach hundreds of thousands of aficionados without compromising the all-important discovery factor.

To this day, Patrón has carefully maintained a profile that is associated with only the finest and most desirable people, places, and things. The celebrity connection continues and deepens. Dan Aykroyd, a close friend of JP's, recently took over the Canadian distribution rights for Patrón. It wasn't just some celebrity pet project. Dan already had his own wine label as well as top-shelf vodka, so not only is he an appropriate and beloved face for the brand in that market, he knows the business.

TEAM PATRÓN

Beyond the celebrity connection, the green and black signature colors of Patrón continue to decorate A-list events such as the Sundance Film Festival and the MTV music awards. It also shows up in some exciting and unexpected ways. Martin always wanted to extend the brand into other areas of lifestyle and entertainment, and had he lived, he would have seen that dream come true as well. Patrón became a presenting sponsor in the American Le Mans Series, investing in more cars, more racing, plenty of signage, and Patrón-fueled parties.

It just so happens that Ed Brown is a car racer and drives the Patrón Spirits Ferrari F430GT at many of the series events. A longtime proponent of consumer motor sports marketing, he uses the Le Mans series to highlight the brand at that racetrack through oncamera signage and hospitality events at the Club Patrón spectator lounge, which is designed to give upscale Le Mans consumers a greater sense of access to the Patrón lifestyle. In addition, JP's beautiful daughter, Alexis DeJoria, became a professional drag race car driver and competes in a Patrón car that runs on Patrón itself—literally the cleanest fuel there is. Between these cars and JP's own Patrón-emblazoned Harley-Davidson motorcycle, Patrón boasts an entire fleet of vehicles yet stays true to its eco-friendly principles.

TEQUILA EXPRESS

Patrón lays claim to some of the most creative brand extension in the industry. Martin never got to realize his dream of building a Patrón airline, but JP came up with a fabulous alternative. His more earthbound vision of luxury travel includes a 1927 refurbished train car called the Patrón Tequila Express that hooks up to Amtrak and travels the country. Decorated like a maharaja's palace with the finest marble and wood paneling, the train car makes an appearance at various parties from coast to coast, from whistle-stops at the 2012 Republican and Democratic conventions to the Kentucky Derby, where JP and Eloise serve up cocktails to specially invited guests.

The 85-foot train car, which once transported the likes of Clark Gable and President Harry Truman, does not just exist to serve the whim of a billionaire who loves to travel in vintage style. He uses it as a backdrop to raise awareness and funds for charities currently supported by JP and Patrón. In 2010 he traveled to New Orleans on the train car for a two-night food and fund-raising effort in support of the St. Bernard Project, a nonprofit that helps rebuild homes, find jobs, and provide mental health support for the people of New Orleans still affected by Hurricane Katrina.

While corporate philanthropy is nothing new to JP and Patrón, their efforts are not just about cutting checks. JP and the Patrón team are actively involved and committed to both raising funds and being out in the field to participate in and witness the results of their fund-raising efforts. Hand in Hand for Haiti, which is raising money to build a hurricane-proof education complex; Smile Train, which repairs cleft palates and lips for underprivileged children around the world; Malaria No More, which sends mosquito nets to Africa; and Action Against Hunger are just a handful of the many specific and highly effective organizations Patrón supports with both advocacy and fund-raising. In keeping with the Patrón tradition, this is not just about blindly giving to the United Way, as many corporations do. These are well-researched and carefully considered organizations that Patrón's staff members embrace both as employees and as human beings. It's an organic connection that lends that sense of authenticity that today's consumer demands. In JP's words, "success not shared is failure."

GROWTH FACTOR

All these innovative efforts have contributed to a decade of phenomenal growth. Patrón Spirits International's revenues have grown to over a billion dollars a year. Even though Patrón produces only ultra-premium products, today it is the largest generator of revenue of all tequila brands. Patrón effectively transformed the liquor industry, triggering a movement known as the premiumization of brands that has inspired staggering sales in this category.

In a move that underlines the stunning transformation of the tequila market since Patrón came on the scene, in December 2012 the spirit distribution behemoth Diageo decided to bid farewell to Cuervo, the once dominant player in the business. Their 16-year relationship came to an end precisely because Diageo was seeking a more upscale tequila brand, something analysts are calling a wise move.[2]

According to the Distilled Spirits Council of the United States (DISCUS), which tracks the liquor market, the number of nine-liter cases of "ultrapremium" tequila sold more than quadrupled to 1.73 million in 2011, from 497,000 in 2003. In 1997, tequila was the least consumed of all the spirits, a bit player in the industry. Now it is the third largest brand category behind rum and vodka, having displaced cognac and whiskey. With sales consistently growing each year, Patrón has been the primary driver of growth in this fastest-growing liquor category. It was the first spirit brand in its price point to sell over a million cases. Today Patrón accounts for over 70 percent of the ultrapremium tequila market.

It's reached a point where Patrón no longer needs the word *tequila* next to its name. People already know. The brand has achieved iconic status, much to the annoyance of its rivals, according to a recent advertisement by a competing brand owned by one of the corporate giants. In the commercial, an actor from the *Sopranos* series makes a sneering reference to Patrón's packaging, deriding the femininity of the brand, yet the last thing the viewer sees is a close-up of the Patrón bottle. As any fool knows, a picture is worth a thousand words, especially in marketing, so this company effectively gave its competition a free plug. If I were the owner of that brand, I would have fired the ad agency for blowing its budget on raising our profile. But I am sure JP was delighted by the compliment.

BUILT BY LOVE

Since Martin's death, business has been so explosive that Patrón has had to move swiftly to upgrade production and expand capacity. The millions of bottles sold originate from the Hacienda del Patrón in the tiny town of Atotonilco in Jalisco, Mexico, a facility that was conceived and designed by Martin, with Francisco's help, and then built by the Patrón team after Martin's death. A couple of years ago, I received a surprise phone call from Francisco, who was visiting Los Angeles on business. He wanted to see me. Although we'd kept in touch by phone after Martin died, we had not met face to face, and I was deeply moved to see our old friend once again. Over dinner, he told me: "I think we have finally created Martin's dream."

The hacienda is a gorgeous complex that is part factory and part palace that aesthetically captures the grace of Mexico's traditional Old World haciendas, with living quarters, meeting rooms, traditional Mexican kitchens where top chefs prepare meals for the workers, a church, and beautiful grounds with gardens. Patrón is working with the local community to build a school for the children of the town and, of course, the factory workers.

Anyone who ever worked for Martin will tell you he believed in rewarding and treating his employees with kindness and respect, a deeply held conviction that JP and Martin shared. The Hacienda del Patrón was designed for the heart and spirit of the business: Patrón's employees. Making the best tequila in the world requires not only time and skill but also passion and commitment. Patrón is the world's number one exporter of 100 percent agave tequila, and the facility has grown to accommodate the world's demand. But Patrón is still produced in small batches for high quality. Today, over 60 hands touch a single bottle before it is shipped, from the harvesting of the agave to the application of the labels. Each hand-numbered bottle is absolutely unique and perfect as it leaves the hacienda, and Patrón's workers take great personal pride in their product.

But don't let the Old World charm of the hacienda's French colonial facade fool you. It houses state-of-the-art technology.

Several years ago at the distillery, a multi-million-dollar reverse os-mosis plant—the first of its kind in the tequila industry—was com-pleted to reclaim waste water from production. As production has increased, so has the need for limiting the environmental impact. When tequila is made, there is a leftover distillate, or stillage, by-product. Rather than discard this, Patrón has developed a reverse osmosis system that recovers 70 percent of the usable water from the stillage. This recovered water is then used in the facilities' cooling towers and for cleaning and irrigating the hacienda's gardens.

The remaining 30 percent of the stillage is used to treat Patrón's compost area. Tequila, of course, is distilled from the native blue agave plant, but not every part of this desert succulent is used in the distillation process. Instead of disposing of this unused agave as waste, Patrón takes the leftover agave tissue, or bagasse, and mixes it with the concentrated stillage to create compost. This compost is used to grow crops in the hacienda's organic vegetable garden, help-ing provide food for factory personnel and the community. The com-post is also used to fertilize the agave fields and is given free to the town to use in area football fields and other gardens and land areas.

ULTRA-ULTRAPREMIUM

As all aspects of production have continued to evolve, so has the product range. In addition to Pyrat Rum, Ultimat Vodka, another top-shelf brand, was added, although they did not invest in a Pol-ish factory as Martin had. As for the tequila, there are many more brands on the market claiming to be ultrapremium, so Patrón has stayed several steps ahead, offering something for everyone from the diehard fan of the original Silver to the wealthy connoisseur seeking something extra special. Adding to the repertoire of Silver, Reposado, Anejo, Citronge, and XO Cafe is yet another flavored tequila: the XO Cafe Dark Cocoa edition. The company also added Gran Patrón Platinum and Gran Patrón Burdeos lines.

In 2007 Patrón launched its Gran Patrón Platinum, which is created from the best agave of the harvest. The agaves for this tequila are hand selected for their high sugar content, triple distilled, and then rested in oak tanks. One of Patrón's bestselling products, it retails for about $250, a price that was unthinkable when we began the business more than two decades ago.

Most recently, Francisco took what he began with Martin to its logical conclusion with the creation of Gran Patrón Burdeos, a limited-production anejo, or aged, tequila distilled from the finest Weber Blue agave in the region that retails for about $500. Burdeos, which was years in development, is first matured in a blend of American and French oak barrels and aged for a minimum of 12 months. It is then distilled again before it is racked in vintage Bordeaux barrels hand-selected from the great châteaux of France.

"We triple distill this tequila to add a soft, velvet-smooth quality unlike any other spirit," explained Francisco, who personally developed the process.

The new products continue to be painstakingly packaged, including hand-etched lead crystal bottles and silver stoppers housed in elegant wooden, velvet, and satin display cases. Recently, it thrilled me to come across an article about a Patrón limited edition. The stopper was created by fashion designer John Varvatos in the form of a gorgeous guitar head. It looks like they had a lot of fun with that, and again everyone came out ahead.

HONORS AND ACCOLADES

From the aged rum and top-shelf vodka to the simple, clean, and pure Silver that is the foundation of Patrón, Martin's enduring legacy is an all-star lineup of award-winning spirits. Far from diluting what's special about the original Patrón, the standard has been meticulously maintained even as the repertoire has expanded, with each product reinforcing the others. In fact, Patrón's contribution has been widely acknowledged by the industry; in 2004 it became the first spirit to receive the Five Star Diamond Award from the American Academy of Hospitality Sciences.

Despite the phenomenal growth, Patrón is still produced in the same small-batch process that Francisco and Martin perfected all those years ago.

I could not be more proud of the stunning success of the business since my own involvement came to an end. JP and his team nurtured our baby with care, love, and respect, realizing Martin's dream above and beyond anything we could have envisioned in those early years, and for that I am grateful.

To me, Patrón is so much more than just a brand. It represents everything that Martin and I meant to each other. It symbolizes a period in our lives of great happiness and flourishing creativity. It's a testament to the exquisite beauty of the life we shared.

JP, Eloise, and I have continued our fond friendship, and I maintain close ties with some of the company's executives who were there when I was, many of whom I was instrumental in hiring. I suppose you could call me an old friend of the Patrón family, which greets me with warmth and love whenever we have the opportunity to reunite at a Christmas party or anniversary. I am their connection to the past and their reminder of the roots of this extraordinary brand of which they are a part. Even though I am no longer officially connected to the brand, it's a part of me. I will forever be:

"The Widow Patrón."

No Regrets

D URING THE TIME we were apart—before, during, and after the trial—I had some strange sightings of Martin. We never spoke, but I would see him parked outside my house, just sitting there. He never got out of the car. He never walked up to my front door and knocked. Not once. And yet it wasn't like he was trying to be discreet. Driving around in a Ferrari made him more than a little conspicuous. In fact, on several occasions friends and acquaintances would call me and remark on Martin's peculiar vigils, which could often last hours into the night.

He was even there one New Year's Eve when I was in the middle of entertaining some friends and oblivious to his lurking presence. I discovered this only years later, when Caroline told me. Had I known, I'd have almost certainly invited him in for a drink or at least stepped out for a quick toast by his car. It pains me to think of him on the outside, looking in at all those people celebrating while he sat there miserable and alone. No one should spend New Year's Eve that way, especially a gregarious soul like Martin. It was such a stark contrast from the convivial times we had shared together.

When I saw him face to face two years later, I asked him what that was about.

"I don't know. I guess I just wanted to get a glimpse of the dogs," he said.

All that time, Martin never once asked me how our dogs were doing. In fact, he was so neglectful after we split that our beautiful koi fish all died of starvation. Some of them had to have been at least 50 years old. And it wasn't like he'd even have seen the dogs hanging out in the front of my house. The dogs remained in the backyard, completely obscured from view, or inside and impossible to see from the bucket seat of a parked Ferrari. I knew the real reason why he was there. Martin missed me, but he wasn't going to give me the satisfaction of admitting it. After everything he did, I cling to this fact. It tells me that whatever happened between us at the end, he never really stopped caring. He loved me as much as I loved him and always will.

Ever since Martin's death, I never stop wondering why things ended the way they did. Before, during, and immediately after was such a roller coaster ride of joy, desperation, and heartbreak that I wasn't able to step back to see what was truly going on. But now that the dust has settled, I think I know.

It was more than the simple fact that the romance had faded. Even though the bloom was off the rose, we had still been best friends and partners in every sense. There was no reason for that to change. We were officially broken up and in mutual agreement about the fact that it was time to move on, yet Martin still couldn't bear to sleep in a bed without me next to him.

The more I think about it, the more I believe his brother Jon was right. As Martin's delusions of grandeur grew and the more successful he became, he felt the need to keep those who knew him too well at a distance. At the deepest core of his being he had put up a self-protecting wall, and heaven help anyone who got too close and threatened to knock it down.

Building the business and living our lifestyle was all part of the enjoyable game of life for Martin until it got so big that the possibility of losing anything scared the hell out of him. It was like a cancer that spread throughout his being, causing him to mistrust even the one woman who had devoted her life to him.

I wasn't perfect. In a moment of despair, I did strike back once. I was overcome with anger and pain after the trial had ended, when Martin, adding insult to injury, sued me for his legal costs to the tune of $80,000. He'd filled the koi pond in his Windsong office with sand to trick the building inspector, who would certainly not have allowed it. He had also built a beautiful French country guesthouse on the property without obtaining a permit. In my downtrodden state I reported all of this to the city of Santa Barbara, and Martin was forced to pay steep fines. But vengeance did not feel good to me; it's just not who I am. It left me feeling disgusted, with huge regret for letting myself sink to that level.

A decade later, not only am I at peace with everything that has happened, I am grateful. Martin gave me two of the greatest gifts: an all-consuming love that many people don't get to experience even once in a lifetime and a chance to share in his dream. Without him, I would never have experienced the thrilling ride of developing an iconic brand such as Patrón. Playing a part in the history of the greatest tequila that ever was made, marketed, and sold was a privilege and a joy. I don't cry because it's over; I smile because it happened. My soul is all the richer for the experience, and no one can put a price on that or take it away. Yes, the end was horrific, but Martin and I shared 13 glorious years, which were the happiest years of my life. As far as I am concerned, I came out ahead. How could I possibly have regrets?

Of course, Sharon and Len, my closest family, still burn in anger on my behalf. Len still remembers that time the police came to Windsong to escort me off the premises as the worst day of *his* life. When we moved into the house in Montecito and I gave up my business to dedicate myself to Martin and Patrón, Len would take every opportunity to urge me to get something in writing, whether it was equity in the business, a ring on my finger, or some kind of salary.

"Ilana, you're a sharp businesswoman. What are you doing? You'd never advise one of your clients to live this way," he admonished.

"Len, please don't worry about me. I took care of myself once, and I'll do it again if need be."

This conversation went on in various forms for six months until Len finally gave up. He knows how stubborn his little sister-in-law can be.

Even Nina Svele, who was almost as close to Martin as she was to me, had her opinion about my situation. A few times she asked me why I wasn't putting aside money for myself, and I scolded her for being so cynical.

"I have no use for money," I'd reply. "You see how Martin and I are; money is just not an issue."

No one understood, then or now. One of the first things they notice about me is that I am nobody's fool. They point out that I am scrupulously fair and compassionate in all my dealings with people, both personal and professional, yet I don't tolerate any nonsense. If something does not seem equitable, I fight like a tigress to make it right. By any measure I am a tough adversary in business and meticulous about how contracts are drawn and deals are made. I will not walk away from the table until I am absolutely certain that all involved, including me, receive a fair and equitable deal in which everyone wins, and then I will follow up and execute relentlessly. Of course, with Martin that was not the case.

To this day, people still ask me: Would you have asked for more? Would you have requested participation in shares of the company? Would you have demanded a marriage certificate? Would you have insisted on a job title or salary? Don't you have any regrets?

The answer is always no. In retrospect, I might have pursued getting something in writing. Perhaps I would have pushed the idea of getting married a little harder. Or maybe I would have paid closer attention and not been so blindsided by the way it ended. But I would never have chosen to love Martin any less. At the time my faith in him was absolute, and I wouldn't have wanted it any other way.

It was a partnership on all levels. No one held rank, and each did what needed to be done to help the other and create something bigger than we were. It's how we were able to put our souls into the building of our brand without reservation. Ours was the romance that produced the perfect cocktail that was Patrón. Our passion, love, faith, and creativity were the ingredients. I don't believe it could have been all that it was if we hadn't met when we did and been able to draw out the finest qualities in each other. Together we were far, far greater than we could ever have been apart.

At its best, our relationship worked like a perfect symphony. It wasn't about power; there was no jealousy or rivalry between us. It was simply the love of a lifetime on the ride of the century, and except for the grueling court case, I wouldn't change a thing.

Besides, we will always have Patrón.

Marking the Patrón Way

PART I

BE READY FOR WHATEVER THE UNIVERSE HAS TO OFFER

The greatest opportunities can come from out of the blue if you are open to them. You cannot discover anything great with your eyes or mind closed. Martin's senses were alive to the possibilities, so the moment he tasted the original Patrón spirit, he understood perfectly the value of what he had found. Many others would have simply enjoyed a drink, moved on, and forgotten about it. But Martin knew that what he had in his hands was incomparable and that if he felt this way, millions of others would too. You cannot force a great brand into existence, but when it presents itself, you can recognize and respond to the opportunity and be prepared to make the most of this monumental gift.

PRESENTATION BROADCASTS YOUR MESSAGE

Packaging must creatively, truthfully, and precisely reflect the quality and experience of its contents. Design is not just a look; it also creates an emotion in your consumers. Martin and I understood that to differentiate Patrón in the marketplace, we had to surround it with a sense of occasion. This unique product uses only the finest ingredients, so the bottle needed to have an artisanal one-of-a-kind look with handblown and etched glass. But we took it a step further, borrowing freely from other industries and applying the best ideas where they were most relevant. In our case, it was the perfume industry, where the detail and quality of the packaging beyond the bottle conveys that a product is a special gift. It's an approach that makes the difference between an iconic consumer brand such as Coke, Chanel No. 5, even Campbell's Soup and another product that gets lost in the crowd.

A GREAT PARTNERSHIP IS A GIFT

Whether you are lovers, friends, or simply business partners with a profound respect for each other's strengths, a true partnership can make the difference between something that's just good and an enterprise that is a phenomenal success. Martin and JP were different on many levels, but they recognized an entrepreneurial zeal and ability to follow through in each other that made them a powerful team. JP's cool business head, vision, and tactical skills were the perfect complement to Martin's creativity and relentless drive. Equally, Martin and I raised the bar for each other in design and brand building. We made his steady stream of brilliant and original ideas happen through my painstaking eye for detail and our shared devotion to quality and aesthetics. It was never my dream—not everyone has one—but what a gift to be able to jump on your partner's dream and follow it together.

NEVER ALLOW CONVENTIONAL WISDOM TO CONSTRAIN YOU

Sometimes ignorance really is bliss. Of course it's important to know the basics of business, but that doesn't mean you must always go by the book. Don't be afraid to set your own bar. Winners don't limit themselves by an industry's norm. The only way to truly be a breakout success is to block out the noise and listen to your own best instincts. Besides, you can't beat the right combination of common sense and creativity. It seemed to Martin and I that beautiful and informed women should always be associated with a brand like Patrón, which is synonymous with good times and good company. We neither knew nor cared that no one else in the industry was using women at trade shows. Thus, the Patrón Girl was born. Remember, you are just as much the consumer as are the people you are marketing to, so deep down you already know what works.

EVERYTHING AFFECTS THE FINAL OUTCOME

A great brand is a combination of the physical production and the intangible magic of the people who surround it. Learn every stage of your product's journey: the production, packaging, and distribution processes. Become an expert on how it's made, from the raw materials to its landing on the shelf in a store. Not only did this enable Martin to step in and troubleshoot whenever something went wrong, it gave him a much deeper appreciation of what he was selling and who was behind it. Once you have become intimately acquainted with the process, you will realize that a product is the result of all the energy of all those who have touched it along the way. In Patrón's case, that means 60-plus pairs of hands, from the farmers in the agave field to the bartenders who stock it on their shelves. Treat everyone associated with your product, at all levels, with love and respect.

PART II

KNOW WHO THE TRUE TASTEMAKERS ARE AND USE THEM WISELY

Think about how all the people in your orbit, whether they are friends, members of the media, or product reviewers, can be best leveraged to promote your product. Celebrities in particular can be powerful tools in brand building. In the consumables business, word of mouth from fashionable and hip brand ambassadors speaks volumes to the mass market. But never, ever try too hard. The cachet of a brand must be organic. Martin quickly realized that we didn't have to chase because we possessed the right relationships, a confident attitude, and a product people were genuinely passionate about. When you have those assets, marketing and promoting a consumer brand doesn't have to cost six figures. And remember, not every star or movie vehicle is appropriate. Be selective about who represents you. At the same time, do not go after one particular market segment. Be inclusive.

NEVER FORGET THE FRONT LINES

Equally if not more important are the people who come into direct contact with the end customer. In our case, that included bartenders, wait staff, restaurateurs, and retailers. Everywhere we went, Martin and I would introduce ourselves with a bottle of Patrón in hand and buy the bar staff a shot of the finest on their shelves. Tasting is believing, so it was the best way to introduce people to the brand and educate them about how it was different and the way it was to be served and consumed. It also assured that we were remembered. Within months, the entire Los Angeles area knew us as Mr. and Mrs. Patrón, which was unique in an industry where there is rarely a live person behind the brand. It's what the best salespeople do: build personal relationships. People appreciated our individual attention, and that helped us stand out in a crowded spirit category.

YOU ARE ALWAYS YOUR OWN
BEST BRAND AMBASSADOR

The best way to promote your brand is to let it infuse every aspect of the way you live. Martin and I followed our passions and brought Patrón along with us. Whether it was yachting, playing polo, or simply throwing spectacular dinner parties for our many friends and acquaintances, Patrón was there. Even our private events were festooned with green and black branding, and all the meals we cooked and the drinks we served involved Patrón as an ingredient or a perfect complement. Outside our home, we were careful to represent Patrón wherever we went, wearing stylish swag and carrying bags emblazoned with our branding so that thousands of pairs of eyes would notice. We had our friends do the same and had them ask for Patrón in every shop, bar, and restaurant, even in states where we did not have distribution. It had a ripple effect that became significant and helped generate huge demand. In a sense, we were cultivating our own authentic narrative for the brand. Our loyal customers did the rest.

EXPECT PROBLEMS ALL THE WAY
DOWN THE LINE

Be as flexible as possible, addressing each issue as it arises. Do not assume someone else will take care of it. Martin frequently flew down to Jalisco to handle even the most mundane production glitch in person.

Of course, he had Francisco to help him, but the fact that Martin owned the brand did not mean he was above staying in the trenches even as the business was growing. In creating an iconic product, you set the standard, and it is only by remaining hands-on and keeping your finger on the pulse that you can keep it as high as it should be.

SOME THINGS WILL ALWAYS REMAIN OUT OF YOUR CONTROL

There is plenty you can do to insulate your business against negative external forces. When the tequila industry got screwed by the worst agave shortage in years, exacerbated by hoarding, crop disease, environmental damage, and changing farming practices, it was something we could not have predicted or changed. However, we were able to turn an industry disaster into an advantage with long-term relationships and sound planning. We survived because we had secured our source, even though it cost more, and consistently delivered quality to our customers when the competition was cutting corners. In addition, we maintained low overheads and enough liquidity to respond to the changing market through brand expansion.

PART III

CONSISTENCY OF QUALITY BUILDS LASTING BRAND LOYALTY

This is the most crucial element of a consumable brand. There will always be temptations to cut corners. Martin faced tremendous pressure to compromise on quality. Seagram's executives tried hard to convince him that the customer cared only about the bottle, not what was inside, but he knew better. During the agave shortage, we'd already seen how hundreds of boutique tequila brands fell by the wayside when they resorted to improperly cultivated agave to maintain production volumes. There was no way Martin was going to accept burnt-tasting tequila just because Seagram's wanted to make more of it in giant steel vats. Never be distracted from the fundamental fact that everything that is great and differentiating about your product should be maintained and always exceed expectations. Remember, you are your own best customer, so follow your own high standards.

IN BUSINESS, YOU *ARE* YOUR REPUTATION

Stand up for yourself. Martin was absolutely correct to challenge Seagram's for keeping our brand off the shelves in a thinly disguised effort to shrink our revenues. He knew they wanted to buy Patrón and were doing all they could to keep our revenues low so that they could get us at a bargain price. But it was a case of David against Goliath. Assume from the outset that the big boys have got you outlawyered and outgunned. That doesn't mean you shouldn't play, but know it's not a fair game. Therefore, negotiate rather than litigate if you possibly can. Do all that you can to keep it out of court. Settlements are less stressful and less expensive in the big picture.

A FRESH APPROACH CAN TAKE YOUR BUSINESS THROUGH THE STRATOSPHERE

There's value in doing what's always worked in the past, but know the difference between consistency and clinging to the old ways. What Martin achieved in his lifetime with no more than a dozen employees was extraordinary. He laid the foundation for the liquor behemoth that Patrón is today. But he was reluctant to loosen his grip and entrust more of the decision making to some of the best minds in the business. After his death, JP and his team took Martin's legacy and ran with it, revamping the marketing message and dedicating millions more in resources to advertising campaigns, promotional events, and distribution coverage, making sure Patrón was available in every bodega, bar, and duty-free store from Maine to Morocco. That's why Patrón is the largest generator of revenue of all tequila brands on the market today. Martin would be proud.

ONCE ESTABLISHED, KEEP THE BRANDING MESSAGE SIMPLE

Let the greatness of your iconic product speak for itself. Doing away with the Bunnies and making Patrón the star of its own advertising campaign was the appropriate decision at the time, because by then it was already well understood that this is the finest ultrapremium in the world. "Simply Perfect" said it all. As Daymond John points out, there is no need to try too hard. Discerning and influential consumers such as the hip-hop community appreciate a brand that builds organically through word of mouth and educated connoisseurs. This is how we established ourselves from the beginning without ever going after any one particular market segment, ignoring the conventional wisdom of business schools with our open architecture marketing. When you create something that is as sublime as it is aspirational, there is no need to chase. Legions of devoted consumers will follow.

Notes

CHAPTER 2

1. http://www.tequilaexperts.com/tequilahistory/index.htm.
2. http://www.goddessaday.com/mayan/mayahuel.
3. http://www.ianchadwick.com/tequila/history.htm.
4. http://www.loscabosguide.com/tequila/tequila-history.htm.
5. http://www.loscabosguide.com/tequila/tequila-history.htm.
6. http://www.ianchadwick.com/tequila/16–17th%20centuries.htm.
7. http://www.tequilaexperts.com/tequilahistory/index.htm,
   http://www.ianchadwick.com/tequila/16–17th%20centuries.htm.
8. http://www.tequilaplanet.com/Learn_tequila.htm.
9. http://www.loscabosguide.com/tequila/tequila-history.html.
10. http://www.tequilawisdom.com/josecuervotequila.html.
11. http://en.wikipedia.org/wiki/Tequila.
12. http://www.tequilasource.com/.
13. http://www.tequilaexperts.com/tequilahistory/index.htm.
14. http://www.shankennewsdaily.com/index.php/2012/04/12/2858
    /Patrón-tequila-picks-up-steam-heads-toward-2m-cases/.
15. http://www.reuters.com/article/2011/08/02/us-tequila
    -usa-idUSTRE7711RL20110802.

CHAPTER 3

1. http://www.alcademics.com/2009/10/drinks-with-francisco-alcaraz
   -of-patron-tequila.html.
2. http://www.alcademics.com/2009/10/drinks-with-francisco-alcaraz
   -of-patron-tequila.html.
3. http://www.ianchadwick.com/tequila/fermentation.htm.
4. http://www.alcademics.com/2009/10/drinks-with-francisco-alcaraz-of
   -patron-tequila.html.
5. http://www.alcademics.com/2009/10/drinks-with-francisco-alcaraz
   -of-Patrón-tequila.html.
6. http://blogs.houstonpress.com/eating/2011/11/a_chat_with_tequila_master
   _fra.php.
7. http://www.islandconnections.com/edit/dejoria.htm.

CHAPTER 4

1. *Daily Variety*, October 29, 2004.

CHAPTER 6

1. http://www.ianchadwick.com/tequila/shortage.htm.
2. http://ministryofrum.com/forums/archive/index.php/t-791.html.
3. All the details of the Seagram's case are part of public court records, but do include the recollections of the author.

CHAPTER 8

1. http://www.businessweek.com/stories/2007–09–16/the-barroom -brawl-over-patrón.

CHAPTER 9

1. http://www.thedrinksbusiness.com/2012/10/Patrón-fuels-growth-with -travel-retail-surge/.
2. http://www.bloomberg.com/news/2013-01-30/diageo-shifting-to -upscale-tequila-after-adios-to-cuervo.html.

Index

About the Author

S HE WAS BORN on the other side of the world from the glamorous celebrity scene of Hollywood, but Ilana Edelstein was destined to be "Mrs. Patrón," the other half of the world's leading brand of luxury tequila that would transform the liquor industry. Together with Martin Crowley, she led the charge in raising the level of perception about tequila by carefully crafting, educating, and marketing the brand, thus initiating an ultrapremium category. For example, they invented the concept of sipping tequila like a fine cognac. Thanks to their revolutionary approach, the pair was the driving force that made tequila the fastest growing category, and "premiumization" has become the norm across all varieties of liquor, from vodka to rum.

Creative and street-smart, the stunning young blonde with the piercing blue eyes made her way to the United States from her native South Africa more than three decades ago through sheer grit and determination, landing on these shores with nothing but her clothes and $200 in savings. Self-reliant and willing to do whatever was necessary, she succeeded in building her own thriving business as a financial advisor before connecting with the love of her life, Martin Crowley, making her the perfect helpmate to build Patrón tequila into the iconic brand it has become.

The child of an Auschwitz survivor, she was raised in Johannesburg under apartheid. She'd lived a sheltered life, studying and winning competitions as a dancer until her parents died three months apart from each other. She was just 18. At that time, most South African youths lived at home until they were married, but Ilana was left abruptly on her own, numbed by grief and struggling to run her family's ladies' clothing shop before closing the business to take an administrative job at a record label.

It wasn't long before her world began to feel too small. A stint of globetrotting a few years later opened her eyes and ignited her sense of adventure. Ilana wasn't political. Behind closed doors her inner circle was multiracial, and she defied government segregation rules by dining and socializing with black and Indian friends and colleagues from the music industry. But her older sister, Sharon, and brother-in-law, Len, the only family Ilana had left, began to fear their two young children wouldn't have much of a future under South Africa's racist regime, so they joined the brain drain and immigrated to Los Angeles. Ilana soon followed, making a dramatic entrance to her wild life in America with an arrest by federal authorities at JFK airport.

There'd been no apparent reason for taking Ilana out of the immigration line. But they found some shipping documents when they searched her luggage and concluded that she was in violation of her tourist visa. Sharon and two baby nephews, who were traveling with Ilana at the time, knew enough to demand their day in court. After several frantic phone calls to Len in Los Angeles, doing their best to console two screaming babies after their 24-hour flight, the sisters located an ace immigration lawyer in New York. The attorney got Ilana a six-month reprieve from a friendly judge, allowing her just enough time to find employment and change her immigration status or go back home. It was her first brush with the U.S. court system; this time justice was served.

As far as she was concerned, returning to South Africa simply wasn't an option. With her polished style, exotic accent, and stunning good looks, she soon talked her way into a job as an assistant to Norman Winter, one of the most powerful image makers in Hollywood at the time. The publicity legend, who repped Michael Jackson, agreed to sponsor her for a green card in exchange for working for a meager $120 a week. For the next five years, Ilana repaid him by working long hours and doing whatever needed to be done to keep his office running. In return, she was introduced to the decadent world of drugs, parties, and celebrity. This shy South African girl who grew up without a television and who was unimpressed by fame was suddenly thrust into the epicenter of Hollywood life at the height of the disco era, when cocaine and Quaaludes were distributed around the office like Post-it notes. Her indifference to the trappings of Tinseltown was irresistible to the many stars circling in her orbit.

Although she enjoyed the parties and general insanity, Ilana chafed at the idea of marking time in an office all day. She had no Hollywood ambitions, although she did possess a strong entrepreneurial streak. When Len, who by then was running his own office supply retail outlet, offered her the chance to be his sales rep and build up his commercial office operation, she quit her PR job to pound the pavement—literally—canvassing every office, law firm, and movie studio that would let her past its gate or reception desk. Within months, she'd built up the business, networking and building relationships with Fox Studios and other major clients around town.

"I quickly realized that in America, everything really *is* bigger, especially the opportunities," recalls Ilana. "The dollar amounts were like phone numbers."

It wasn't long before Ilana's sales business was running itself. With an extraordinary facility for numbers, she then turned her attention to finance and built up an advisory business for teachers looking to invest their retirement funds. By the time this flourishing businesswoman met her life partner, she had more than 700 clients and was netting more than a quarter of a million dollars a year.

The rest of Ilana's story is the story of Patrón. This unsung heroine in building up a brand that changed the face of the liquor industry was involved every step of the way, from the ingenious and unprecedented marketing strategies to each complex detail of its finance and operations. Patrón and the lifestyle associated with the brand became synonymous with Ilana and Martin and the powerful connection they shared. There was no separation between the two or the business of Patrón that they nurtured together.

"We were all one," says Ilana.

Ilana had been asked to give up her business to focus on Martin and Patrón, and she did so willingly. She walked away with little but the integrity and self-respect she prizes above everything else. And she'd do it all over again.

Despite what he put her through, she looks at the time she shared with Martin as a gift. She faced her hardship and humiliation with a quiet dignity, strength, and compassion. The sadness of their demise notwithstanding, she reflects back on the man he was with empathy and chooses to focus only on the many good memories of the love of her life. Meanwhile, she's rebuilt her financial consulting business beyond where it was, living a comfortable albeit slightly less wild life in West Los Angeles with her two dogs and her cat and maintaining close ties with her beloved family and many friends.

She still dances, she still creates, and she still drinks only Patrón.